Tales from Lyla's Log

Tales from Lyla's Log

Adventures aboard a cruising sailboat from Cape Cod to Florida and the Bahamas

by Harry Jones

Dead
Reckoning
Publishing

Copyright 2010
Harry Jones
All Rights Reserved
Dead Reckoning Publishing
1132 Calle de los Amigos
Santa Barbara, California 93105
ISBN: 1-453-76875-0
Printed in the USA
Sailing/Travel/Adventure

First Edition

To Ginger

Contents

Introduction	1
Chapter One: Finally, we get under way	9
Chapter Two: Busy summers on The Vineyard	109
Chapter Three: A long thrash to windward	113
Chapter Four: The trip begins with a big clean-up	119
Epilogue	179
Glossary	181
Charts:	183
1: Cape Cod to Alligator River	184
2: Albemarle Sound to Daytona Beach	185
3: Florida and the Bahamas	186–187

Chart diagrams and courses in this book are for reader orientation—not navigation.

Introduction

In early 1970, after 20 years in the design business, I decided that the time had come to move on to other endeavors. My business partners bought me out and subsequently I landed a position to run a small firm called Vineyard Yachts which would entail moving to Martha's Vineyard Island in Massachusetts. The previous ten years had been spent building and living in a house I'd designed in the countrified outskirts of New Canaan, Connecticut, while my two partners and I created and expanded a company called Product Development Services, Inc.

For fun, during those years, I took up sailing and before long I was asked to crew on a friend's big, beautiful Concordia yawl, and *that* led to crewing on several other Concordias which competed in two- or three-day races along the New England coast each summer. The men on these boats, as much as twenty years my senior, were old-time traditionalists who took their sailing seriously. Thus I'd happened upon a great opportunity since there is no better way really to learn this sport than to crew with skilled sailors pushing, say, a forty-footer to its utmost limits (sometimes beyond), unremittingly, day and night, in calm and in storm. After some years of such experiences one is quite prepared for the vicissitudes of cruising, and that became the aspect of the sport which most intrigued me.

New Canaan was a fine place to live especially because many of my wife Ginger's relatives lived in the area—lots of cousins' parties. But as the years passed, budding careers forced one family after another to move away while, at the same time, suburbia was closing in on us. One day I stepped out of the house for some fresh air and inhaled 50% exhaust fumes. A month later a new, red/amber/green traffic signal appeared at the end of our street. "That's *it!*" I said to Ginger, and she agreed, "It's time to move."

Thus began the process that landed us on the Vineyard to become 100% mixed up with "messing about in boats." By the summer of 1970 we'd sold our house (after I'd put the last few pieces of trim in the master bath) and moved to Vineyard Haven where both of us became involved with the manufacture and selling of thirty-two foot, fiberglass, sport-fishing boats patterned after a down-east style lobster boat. In what little time we could spare from the new job we'd leave work a little early and sneak off in our 27-foot sloop for a quick sail before dark. While heading back into the harbor I often thought, "I don't want to go in. What if I didn't turn back and just kept going? What would it be like to sail off to far places?" I began to dream; might a long-term cruise actually be possible for us? Would I, and would Ginger, thrive on such a life for many months? What would the boat be like? What must it be capable of? How had others done it? Too often they seemed to suffer too much; how could we do it more enjoyably?

Never did either of us have big ideas about blue water cruising, crossing oceans and the like. Rather it was always coastal cruising that would include two or three days at sea now and then. Occasionally we'd spend a weekend cruising Cape Cod, gunk-holing up one little creek to some cove and then the next morning perhaps squeezing through a shallow passage to another picturesque creek. But Sunday evening always we had to return and I'd get that urge again. It was just a momentary thing before the real world would take over as we put the boat on its mooring and rowed home in the dinghy.

One day that urge abruptly became an idea. Might it be possible to do it? Naah, no way. Number one: we couldn't afford it. We'd need a much bigger boat. How could we possibly buy, run and maintain that bigger boat plus pay all the other costs of cruising on top of basic living expenses?

A month later the idea was back. Might it be possible to find a thirty-five-footer in poor condition and rebuild it for little more than what our very marketable Cheoy Lee sloop might sell for? Could the financial roadblocks be circumvented by broad application of do-it-yourself? By the time I'd spent a year rebuilding that boat, I'd know it so well that I could do all the maintenance too. But what boat? That was the first, big, complicated unknown to be investigated among many others. Would it be a wooden boat or fiberglass? Much as I admired the lines and exquisite joinery of a Concordia, or was thrilled by the several schooners and other classics in Vineyard Haven's harbor, I knew that I could afford only fiberglass. It wasn't until much later that I realized how fortunate I was to have had those years of training on the Concordias, and then to have taken up fiberglass as a business. Both experiences made it far easier to sort out the fine points of cruising at a time of great changes in sailing, exceeding all those of the last hundred years.

First, the change from wooden boats to fiberglass brought about a huge decrease in the cost of boats because the fiberglass process so efficiently lent itself to mass production. A boat big enough to cruise in suddenly became affordable by a significant portion of American citizenry. Shortly thereafter, sailing gear, construction materials and methods began to change from those traditionally found in wooden yachts to new thinking which fell under the compelling influence of high tech.

Think back to 1975. Taffrail logs typically still measured distance, celestial navigation and chronometers still were required for blue water passages. (Someone was about to realize that three cheap quartz-crystal watches could out-mode the chronometer.) There was no GPS; Loran was in its infancy and cost thousands; only unreliable radio-direction-finders were in broad use. Depth sounders with consistent readings in less than six feet were very expensive, VHF radio just in, was intermittent at 40 miles, roller furling jibs were untrustworthy. Concerns about the strength of fiberglass arose as vessels came apart in the heavier storms because sufficient experience was lacking and proven layup methods were just being established to define new, "glass" scantlings. Marine epoxy, only a few years earlier, had achieved adhesive strength previously inconceivable. It was also not only completely waterproof but sealed out even water vapor.

All this meant that many new sailors with limited (or no) experience had a great deal to learn. In order to sell these new boats, sales pitches often implied "no experience necessary," which made these sailors not only subject to many failures but also resulted in many of them going to sea devoid of piloting skills and ignorant of the rules of the road as well. The demand for reliable information thus produced was so pervasive that the forty-odd-year-old nautical bible, known as

Chapman's, in its 1968-69 edition, felt compelled to add some eleven new chapters and many more new features in order to meet the needs of these sailors.

In these early years, "glass" boat designs often imitated the shapes of wooden boats and for good reason. With a hundred years of development and tradition behind them, wooden sailing yachts had reached a state of perfection in both speed and graceful appearance culminating in what became known as the "Classic Cruising Club of America Look." For years I had admired the mahogany and oak yacht, *Finisterre*, a lovely, 39-foot, keel-centerboard yawl. I read everything I could find about her, including her owner Carleton Mitchell's instructions to his naval architects, "First, I want a floating home for two people and, second, she must be able to win some races."

The designers replied, "She'll have to be beamy to carry all your homey stuff but maybe we can use that beaminess to enable her to stand up under lots of sail which will drive her through seas that would slow other boats." *Finisterre* went on to win three Bermuda Races in a row!

So it was with *Finisterre* in mind that Ginger and I began to arrive at a concept of what we really wanted a boat to be. First, a boat for the two of us to live on for long periods and thus one which could accommodate the amenities of comfortable living. A boat having such capacity would be about forty feet overall in wood, but in fiberglass this space could be found in a thirty-five-foot hull. The cost saving of the smaller boat might make the whole project possible. Decision made; I'll search for an older, beamy, fiberglass boat.

I had to agree with those who think that "glass" boats often look like plastic toys. And thin, glass hulls sweat in cold weather attracting mold. Soon the blankets are so damp that one's bunk is clammy to climb into—not fun, night after night. Our boat must have the look, feel and even the odor of fine wood, especially down below. The hull would be glass, but many thick layers of it. The deck should have a balsa-wood core laminated between layers of glass—absolutely leak-proof, but light and very stiff. Nothing ruins the first night of a cruise more than curling up in your bunk under a wooden deck and discovering water dripping slowly from overhead. I would insulate the entire interior of the hull with quarter-inch, closed-cell foam eliminating the sweating and then finish it in varnished wood with every structural detail like those in a fine wooden boat. WEST Epoxy© (explicitly formulated for use in boats) would make it all significantly stronger. However, wooden boat interiors finished entirely in one type of wood are often dark so our bulkheads below will be traditional, vertically-V-planked, and painted white. Now I had to find a boat to rebuild with the right underlying characteristics.

Several times we went sailing with a friend on his fiberglass, 33-foot Rhodes Swiftsure. It's a pretty boat, handles well and is heavily built and rigged. At times she'd nicely sail herself. Several hundred of them had been sold since they appeared in 1959 so used Swiftsures must be available. What's more she was a product of the famous naval architect, Phillip Rhodes, known especially for his success at designing shallow-draft, keel-centerboarders, just right for sailing in the shallow Intracoastal Waterway (ICW). But down below she was a total mess. Absolutely hopeless! Only a rudimentary galley, not a single place to sit comfortably—and she smelled moldy.

Months went by as I researched other fiberglass boats, when all at once my idea crystallized. An entire, new interior for the Swiftsure popped into my head in considerable detail. Now, as a designer, I was always dreaming up something, and all too often I've had inspirational ideas which seemed wonderful but rarely survived the light of morning. This one kept reappearing and always with a rush of enthusiasm. I'd think, "Wouldn't it be neat if...?" On an impulse, one day, I called Phillip Rhodes' office in New York to ask if I could buy stock plans of their Swiftsure. To my surprise they sent me a set and somehow forgot to charge me! It turned out that they had always been disgusted with this boat's interior which, they said, had not been designed by them but by the client's marketing department! I laid tracing paper over their drawings and began at once to create the new interior. Everything seemed to fit! She would be just big enough, and the ideas were really going to work.

I did some cost figuring. "Wouldn't it be neat" (again) to sail away some October and not come back until June? We could rent the house. We know several couples who live in summer-only houses and need a winterized place each winter. *They* would have to pay the heating bill, not us. Our car, left in the garage for seven months would cost us almost nothing while the boat's engine would burn little more than a half gallon per hour. Cruising all winter might not cost much more than staying home!

I put an ad in *Soundings* magazine. "Wanted: one Swiftsure which needs work," and the replies began to come in. My close friend, Pat West, a veteran marine surveyor, taught me how to run a survey on a Swiftsure. Not how to survey any boat, of course, but just the Swiftsure. Eventually I drove long distances to survey four of them.

I'd gone all the way to Annapolis to survey the fourth which was a dud. But just as I was finishing, and six tons of boat was being lowered back into the water, the boatyard's loudspeaker called my name. It was Ginger on the telephone saying that a man with a Swiftsure for sale had called from just north of Falmouth, only an hour from home.

My Cheoy Lee had recently sold, so after a week of telephone dickering, I had to add only $900 to the cash I'd just received to buy this Swiftsure. Although it was 18 years old (typical) it was in good shape with a beautiful, newly refinished, wooden mast and a replacement engine with only 25 hours on it. The fiberglass hull had been repainted poorly by an amateur and that, along with the horrible, standard interior and cash that I waved in the owner's face forced the price way down. I couldn't have been more excited. I knew I could *fix* that boat.

The first weekend that we could break from work we set out on a two-day planning cruise. Didn't matter where we went. Our minds were completely on that boat! What changes in the rig would make it easier for the two of us to handle? Just how did Ginger want the new galley? Where would we plan spaces for a hundred different items? Should we build this, or, we must have that. An interior that had been designed to sleep six people was now to be re-built for the comfort of just the two of us plus two guests in a pinch. Above all, Ginger demanded, "It has to be civilized." (Meaning such features as a gas stove with oven, pressurized hot water, a shower and some sort of compact heater to keep us warm.)

This remark became our mantra for two years of work in every spare minute. Now I could proceed to replace the very narrow, fiberglass, cabin trunk and apply all I had recently learned about the technique of joining wood to fiberglass. The entire cabin trunk was sawed off at the deck line, taken to the dump, and replaced with one of mahogany a foot wider. The interior was torn out until there was little left except the engine inside the bare hull and I could insulate every inch of it.

When *Lyla* was finally finished in the fall of 1983 every detail was just as *we* wanted it. ("Lyla" is an old-French corruption of *L'isla*—"from the island.") Everything worked and was strong, leak-free and rot-free. Every feature was there for comfortable living be it cold, hot or stormy. There are thirteen drawers, each with a lift-lip and not one of them ever jams. The galley has lots of counter space and lockers, a stainless sink and a two-burner propane stove with oven, on gimbals. A propane, instant hot-water heater supplies galley and head. A specially designed Aladdin cabin heater will keep us warm and dry out the cabin. There are more than seven feet of dry bookshelf.

To port, outboard of a settee, is a pilot-berth where one can sleep on either tack when the boat is rail down in a heavy sea. To starboard, another berth slides out to 40 inches wide. Up forward the two vee-berths can be wider in port or high-sided and narrow at sea. We can live aboard without being connected to anything. All the equipment for all kinds of sailing has been acquired and now is properly built in. Even her appearance is markedly improved. And yes, down below she looks and smells like a wooden boat with teak and varnished mahogany—even thin, cherry "ceiling-strips" cover the insulation alongside each bunk. We are so proud of her! What follows is a story fleshed out directly from the three hundred pages of *Lyla's* logbook.

Chapter One
Finally, we get underway

SUNDAY, OCTOBER 23, 1983: We've been trying to leave for two days now but of course there are details upon details yet to be accomplished. Even though *Lyla* was launched three months ago there remain many unfinished essentials down below in the cabin. For instance, last week the depth sounder, speed indicator, and VHF radio were still in their boxes in the house, and necessities such as a bracket not yet built to hold the centerboard crank-handle at the ready, and a chart table light yet to be bought and installed, et cetera. The house is rented and the renters spent last night with us getting clued in. Business opportunities have been closed down, and we have no intention to come back before sometime in May of next year.

The first part of the trip south will be in familiar waters, but after we leave Cape May, New Jersey, each day will be in a place we have never seen before. The days are already getting short and cold, so the weather will force us often to omit potentially interesting side trips. We can't expect to find warm winter weather until we are well south of the Florida line and that is more than a thousand miles away.

Lyla is lying at the town dock just below the house loaded with more stuff than it seems we could ever need. Ginger has just brought down 30 pounds of ice and a load of food for the ice box as I try to get the wiring finished. Finally, at 1115 hours we cast off. Whew!

It's cool as we motor out of the harbor, about 60° with a weak winter sun in a gray sky. A light wind out of the ENE ruffles the water. Halfway to West Chop, I get up the mainsail and then we set the big genoa jib. With the engine just idling we are quickly up nearly to hull-speed. Giving West Chop a wide berth to avoid the nasty, confused, steep seas for which the point is named, we set a course across Vineyard Sound to Woods Hole on a nice broad-reach.

Our druthers would have been to go southwest down the sound but its powerful current had turned foul against us several hours ago so we must go straight across, through Woods Hole where the current will be near slack instead of treacherous, and then turn southwest down Buzzard's Bay where, weirdly, the current will be fair. We know all this because, as every sailor around here must, we consult the famous *Eldridge Tide and Pilot Book* before going anywhere. It shows what the currents are doing each hour of each day for the entire year in every square yard of water from Boston to Bridgeport.

Our destination for the night is Point Judith in Rhode Island about 35 miles from Woods Hole. By the time we'd made the turn to southwest coming out of Woods Hole the wind had piped up giving us a nice ride all the way. A little before 10 PM we spotted the breakwater lights at the narrow harbor opening and half an hour later slid into the so-called "Harbor of Refuge." In spite of the long breakwaters which surround this place there's always a roll here so we moseyed around a bit in the pitch darkness before anchoring. Sitting in the cockpit for a few minutes, with the boat secured, we notice the wind has dropped… and all is quiet…not another boat in this huge place.

Suddenly, SMOKE BELOW! Billowing out of the companionway! I dive below smelling electrical wiring. Turned out to be the freshwater pump which I'd left un-fused in my rush to finish. Fortunately there is a foot pump built in below the galley sink so we can draw water but the pump must be replaced. It's been a busy day.

MONDAY, OCT. 24: Last night was only slightly rolly. Too bad we have no time to go sight-seeing up in the pond but winter's coming. Temperature still comfortable with jackets. Not glove weather yet. Gray, broken clouds with weak sunlight. High, 50°, low 36.

It feels great to be off on our big adventure. *Lyla* is crammed with stuff that will take weeks to stow. We feel very much equipped and ready for whatever's ahead. Why does fall have such a strong feeling of finality? We're going to sail away from that, and right now we're off down the Rhode Island coast. Figured Mystic Shipyard would be the best place to get the necessary pump. At long last we've satisfied my former craving by sailing out of Vineyard Haven Harbor with no need to return! I'm reminded of the emotions of leave-taking from land and shore life described by Joseph Conrad, I believe, in *Lord Jim*. Glad this breeze is on our quarter—there's conviction in the way it blows. Comfortable sailing, nearly rail-down. Feels like heavier weather coming.

TUESDAY, OCT. 25: We are in Mystic Shipyard having blown in here about 3 PM yesterday as it was breezing up to 25 knots or so. This morning it's blowing harder, gray and wintery-feeling out on the docks, so it's nice to be staying put as we wait for the pump to be delivered. Also I'll be glad that we're in a sheltered slip when I have to lie flat on the cabin sole in order to reach into a space under the stove while installing the pump—correctly this time with an inline fuse.

This big shipyard is battened down for winter! Its life has all turned inward; almost no one is visible. A lone figure scurries by, hunched against the wind, his coat-collar blown up around his ears. A door bangs distantly. Dozens of boats in and out of the water are hidden under tight, canvas covers. The insistent sound of halyards clanging against aluminum masts is blown away by a powerful gust. Helped Chris McLaughlin move his West 38, a stripped-down, racing machine, from one slip to another. Some quick work with the mooring lines so as not to lose control of it in the wind. Then back to our warm cabin with it's Aladdin heater. Perhaps Sachem's Head tomorrow.

WEDNESDAY, OCT. 26 (my birthday)*:* We really made good time today with fair current. Our early start put us off Sachem's just after noon so decided to push on to Norwalk, Connecticut (30 miles) since we could easily navigate in the dark to an anchorage in our old home waters. We used to sail at night frequently there because the wakes of motor boats had become so dense in Long Island Sound during the day that a sail boat would just bog down, barely able to move forward.

Chilly and partly cloudy, the high for the day was 40°. Light air early, then a good breeze which failed at sundown. Fun to pass all the familiar "landmarks" in the sound. We really didn't need a chart, we know it all so well. Thames River entrance, Fisher's Island Sound, Long Sand Shoal, Cornfield Point at the Connecticut River. New Haven's high breakwater, Stratford Shoal which looks like a submarine in the distance, Bridgeport's industry, Southport, and finally, after dark, the old "spark plug" lighthouse, Green's Ledge Light. There, inshore, was that weak, four-second green flasher at Five-Mile River entrance that one must know exactly where to look before it can be seen. And similarly, the black shadow of the can-buoy halfway in from Green's Ledge which Ginger's cousin, Russ Bradley, used to teach me how to see in the dark. It sits there, silent and motionless, its presence felt more than seen, like some animal which has seen you long since and is…waiting.

We ghosted in among the Norwalk Yacht Club fleet on the departed breeze until we found an empty mooring. We'd check in in the morning (we were former members).

THURSDAY, OCT. 27: Up about eight to light the Aladdin. By the time Ginger had breakfast on, I shut it down as we were getting too warm. Looks like a nice day coming up; about 40°. Dead still right now, and partly sunny for a change. Breakfast is dry cereal, juice, toast, and bacon. Yum. I make up my berth and step up to the cockpit as Ginger begins washing up. Nothing moving in the harbor, no one at the Club float. Less than half the Norwalk Yacht Club fleet, of about thirty sailboats, is still on its moorings all around us. The engine starts instantly—which likely means it's OK—and I amble forward to drop the mooring. A glance around the deck and rig shows nothing out of place. Picked up the tiller, kicked her into gear and we're off for Five-Mile River and the town of Rowayton just a mile away.

If you've ever been in the Five-Mile River you'll know why we didn't barge in there in the dark last night, but now we need to be more accessible to hardware, market, bank and guests. This little river is jammed with boats on private moorings squeezing the narrow channel from both sides for half a mile up stream. One shore is a continuous array of floating docks each with a dozen or so slips. The other shore displays the houses of Darien peeking out through the trees. Rowayton is a *place-to-be!*—a village completely dedicated to yachting but built with no plan at all. It was probably most attractive 20 years ago when we kept our first sailboat here. Now, gentrification has brought multi-story condos and expensive shops along its single main street but no longer a single, decent, marine hardware store. However, along the water, it remains a charming example of the classic period after W.W. II when yachting first spread from the very rich to the common man with a few extra bucks.

Ed Raymond's house must still be owned by the Raymonds because his famous *Chanty Man* is in its same old slip. His renowned sail loft made the big genoa for our second boat. We tied up at a long, floating dock astern of *Kate*, a 48-footer out of Edgartown. What a coincidence! We would "speak her" again at the entrance to the Alligator-Pungo Canal in North Carolina.

Melanie, our grown daughter, joined us here and we all had dinner with an old friend in New Canaan. Nice, but also nice to "go home" to the boat. The port berth is still crammed with un-stowed stuff so Mel slept forward that first night. She'll be a necessary third crew on our twenty-eight-hour overnight sail to Cape May, New Jersey.

Russ Bradley came aboard to visit and approve many of *Lyla*'s details. Years ago he and his wife, Cornelia (Ginger's cousin) took us on our first sailing cruise from Maine to Vineyard Haven. He was thus my first sailing instructor who filled my head not only with the rules of the craft but the fun, beauty, traditions and satisfaction of it.

FRIDAY, OCT. 28: After breakfast, Ginger and Mel went shopping and I worked stowing stuff on board trying to get the boat ready for more serious sailing. The weather report says it's blowing 25 to 35 in the gusts out on the sound and wind out of the southwest means we'll be beating in to it. Departed at 10:15 for the two hour trip to Greenwich where we have more good friends to see.

Took quite a pounding in at least five-foot seas and the dodger leaked a bit at its front edge so we were glad to get in. However, a full-width dodger is an absolute godsend. There couldn't be a better name for it. That's what we did, ducking under it every time the bow dug into the green water of a big wave which would then throw about 20 gallons high in the air to come crashing down on us. It wasn't comfortable but, surprisingly, we stayed almost dry. Up the river in Old Greenwich the water was calm but the wind was shaking the mast, and halyards on other boats were clanging. We pulled into the Texaco dock and made arrangements to spend the night (for $22!). Called the Donalds who came right down. They owned a boat just like our second boat and took us for a demonstration sail when we were trying to decide on the purchase. We've kept up ever since. They gave us a delicious lunch at Riverside Yacht Club. Wouldn't let us share the check. No sooner had they left when Ellen and Jack Wardle came aboard. Conservative Jack quite nervous in disbelief that we could be at all comfortable. Ellen enjoyed it all. (At age 14, she was my first girlfriend.)

Another wintery, gray day and blow-ing! So why don't we just stay put? Well, two reasons. First, the current turns foul at Hell Gate, in New York's East River one hour later each day, and from our push to depart Vineyard Haven when we did, to our long day sailing to Connecticut, to our thrash yesterday, the requirement that we go through Hell Gate with fair current has set a deadline which we must meet or wait a whole week. The second reason is Melanie. She can't hang around with us for more than a few days. We're spending a lot of time seeing friends which is great fun but it's already taken seven days from Vineyard Haven.

Thus we must make City Island tonight and then be under way by first light or 0530 tomorrow morning in order to pass through, during slack, to avoid the worst whirlpools and foaming current surges for which Hell Gate is named, and then emerge into New York Harbor before the current turns strongly against us. Then we'll carry on to Cape May.

Jack appeared again, driving to the outer breakwater to gape and wave as we reached the river's mouth. Long Island Sound was really kicking up, just as it was yesterday, so we must have been quite a sight with all the spray flying.

Again we endured a pounding in the Sound's well known, short, five-foot chop and I began to learn about beamy centerboarders! Must build a coaming to seal the front edge of the dodger. Not another boat in sight.

It's interesting how quickly, at the onset of winter and the retreat of warm sun, that the sea coast is deserted by human beings. They turn their backs and forget all about it 'till spring. Then, in sheltered pockets (boatyards) the joy returns. The present day sailor knows little of this joyous time as he does little of his own work and boatyards are peopled now only by employees. Oh, the old camaraderie when rich man, poor man worked together to ready their boats for another season.

We crashed onward for almost three hours before reaching calmer water in behind City Island, a place next to the Bronx which time has utterly passed by. Through the last half of the nineteenth century this island was crowded with great yacht builders like Nevins and famous sailmakers such as Ratsey. The huge J-boats which defended America's Cup in those days were often built here. City Island is now quietly rotting away. We found plenty of space among many moored boats and picked up a mooring just off City Island Marina where our first boat came from. Its long, high wharves are so rotten that one's foot may break through at any moment.

In 1962, I came here to follow up on a lead I had about a small sailboat that had been damaged in a storm and might be had for a bargain. This marina had once been a large operation covering about six acres but now was nearly closed down. Rows of big, tumbledown sheds, decrepit old vessels in cradles and much open space with junk everywhere. The office was staffed by one lone secretary and the owner who was totally blind. In response to my inquiry about a Corinthian, a model I'd had my eye on, the owner replied, "Ya wanta look at 'er?"

"Yep."

"OK, follow me," he said, picking up his white cane, and out the door he went like a man with full sight, his seeing-eye dog padding at his heels. We headed down between one of the rows of tin sheds till he pulled up pointing to the left with his cane.

"Is there a door there?"

"Yes—?"

"What'sa number on it?"

"Thirty-seven," I said.

He pulled a key ring from his pocket saying, "Here, unlock it." As soon as I'd opened the door, he banged both sides of the opening with the cane and marched inside into total gloom. After perhaps 20 steps he stopped and pointed again. "Is there a boat there? I'm told it's gray-green."

"Yes."

"Well, go have a look and lemmee know what you think. There should be a ladder on the left near the door."

"Where's the mast?" I asked.

"On the rack right beyond her."

A while later I asked, "Where's the outboard?"

"On the left, next to the wall. It's a four-horse Evinrude."

I hadn't noticed it in the dim light. He knew the exact location of every item that belonged to that boat! We bargained and discussed the repairs. New, a Corinthian sold for $3,000. I got it for $500. As I was departing he said, "If you were gonna pay someone else to fix that boat it would've been a thousand." It was to be my first experience with fiberglass.

Back on *Lyla*, it felt a little lonely out in that big anchorage with no one in sight on land or sea. Lots of moored boats but not a soul on any one. No fellow cruisers. The wind is shaking the mast and that weak, gray, winter light is setting the mood again. Partly cloudy, though the sun showed for sunset. To the northeast, Execution Rock stood out gray and sharp with the sun on it two miles away. The temperature is dropping this evening and we expect it to be below freezing before morning. Our Aladdin lamp on the cabin sole keeps us comfortable. Mel and Ginger whipped up a yummy dinner and went to bed early. A note here about Ginger's "civilized" living requirement: we make up the bunks properly with sheets and pillowcases so we sleep well, and our sterling flat-silver on the mahogany table at dinner both glow in kerosene lamplight as neither does under electric light. Things are beginning to get properly stowed. All systems working.

SATURDAY, OCT. 29: We're up before first light with intent to start as soon as we can see. It's cold, well below 32°; but the wind is down and everything is quiet. We're putting on plenty of layers and Ginger got out warm gloves for us. We go about the small tasks of getting the boat ready for today and the overnight to Cape May, stowing loose items, pulling out the charts we'll need. Ginger and Mel start to make breakfast.

It's 5:45 AM when I climb out on deck and go forward to hank on the jib, and it's just getting light as Mel starts the engine and we're off. There will be full light before we get to the tricky part. Ginger hands up breakfast as Mel and I huddle under the dodger to stay out of the headwind. We are treated to a glorious morning as we enter the East River, clear and sunny. The big-city buildings all around us stand out sharply with the rising sun painting the streaks of clouds orange against a cold blue sky. At 34° we're quite comfortable in gloves and hoods.

    The East River is full of hazards; one must keep a sharp eye out and check the charts frequently for submerged rocks and old concrete structures. There are many, often blind, turns in the channel. Each buoy must be identified and honored, tug traffic avoided and their whistle signals heeded. As the river narrows, the current becomes visible rolling the buoys down to extreme angles until they burst free in a frothing wake only to roll down again. When we came upon the first whirlpool, its hundred foot circle looked ominous but we passed through unaffected; the current has already begun to slack. Not a lot of tug traffic at this hour. A big one pushing a much bigger barge, or worse, several at once can really threaten a small sail boat with their powerful wakes.

    Nice panoramic view of the city with many distant sounds of people waking and going to work. All the bridges—the Triborough, the Queensboro, the Manhattan and the Brooklyn—are each impressive as one passes underneath. In the river's southern part, the proper channel must be selected and found. Mel replaces one chart with another as we try to determine which set of buoys leads to which channel before we emerge into Upper Bay where the East River meets the Hudson. It's big compared to the East River and I expected the Verrazano Narrows Bridge to be right in front of us but it takes more than a few minutes before it pops out from around the corner of Brooklyn. As soon as we pass under it we're in New York Harbor which is even bigger, and suddenly container ships, cruise liners, and huge, bulk-cargo ships are bearing down on us at high speed from several directions. One of these can appear sufficiently far away to ignore, but in three minutes it suddenly looms much larger. Will it pass ahead or behind us? It's hard to tell! In another minute it overtakes us in a huge, shuddering rush, towering high above our mast. We've learned to note whether a vessel's angle of approach is increasing or decreasing. It's the one whose angle doesn't change over a minute or so that would run us down. A vessel aimed right at us will actually pass far behind us.

The mainsail's been up all morning but now we have a nice northwesterly breeze and we set the genoa too. What's more, we've carried a fair current all the way. Eventually we spot famous Sandy Hook and identify several New Jersey communities. Sandy Hook is abeam at 10:45 AM so from now till tomorrow, mid-morning, we'll run a mile or two off the unbroken, unremarkable, nearly straight beach of the Jersey shore. Actually this constant beach is broken by several river entrances with long breakwaters projecting out making them dangerous to enter if the wind is against an incoming tide.

Manasquan Inlet is one of these and about the only attraction along this shore. Since it will appear about six o'clock we've decided to pull in for dinner. Some years ago we were there while sailing with Bob Love so we know what to look out for and where the restaurant is. The chart of this area shows a number of interesting looking waterways here but most of this water is too thin for our three and a half foot draft.

The entry is uneventful and we mosey around exploring before tying up at the restaurant. One nestles up to its face dock in any space between other boats and, behind a long line of big windows, there all the diners are eating only about twenty feet away across the boardwalk. Nice! But we locked up before walking in.

Just before dark we were out of there. Up with the main and the genny, and the engine is shut down. Ah, peace and quiet! No need to set formal watches. Mel says she'll stay dressed, ready to come topside if the helmsperson needs help. With one of us on the helm two can sleep whenever. Mel takes to it all so competently that it's easy on both of us. She's the sailor-of-senior-experience-at-sea on board.

I do enjoy the sights and sounds aboard a sailboat at night. The slightly hushed voices in the cockpit overheard when one is below. The rush of water three inches from one's ear when dozing off. The running lights of shipping, the shore lights and the process of identifying them. The sounds of the sails and rig, and of the waves pushed aside by the bow. Watching the first tints of the new day finally arrive. A companion's sleepy appearance in the dark companionway; "Where are we? What's the weather out there?" The smell of bacon frying below smells better than it ever does ashore.

SUNDAY, OCT. 30: At exactly 10 AM we are off the Cape May breakwaters and turning in. Again, this is an easy entry in calm conditions. Cape May is a sizable community of summer houses, an important Coast Guard station, half a dozen marinas which form a base for serious sport fishing, a lighthouse, water and radio towers, a rail center and an airport with four runways. It's all sand and dunes with scant, coarse bushes; obviously a windswept place. The harbor, about two miles long, runs parallel to the Atlantic shore and is separated from it by a wide, flat sand dune. The low dune supports the towers and a number of beach houses which are not infrequently overrun by winter storms. The season here is over and many businesses are preparing to close for winter. The navigable portion of the harbor is very narrow providing little space to anchor but the marinas looked so big and uninviting that we nudged in to one spot just clear of traffic and dropped two anchors positioned to allow us to swing around with wind and tide changes but move little from our spot. We're far from the nearest shore to the east but this will do for one night.

MONDAY, OCT. 31: After a leisurely breakfast, we motored into the marina at the head of the harbor for gas. We'd been told that this marina hates sailboats and surely it was populated by big sport-fishermen, but we were astounded when the dock attendant refused to let us take on water, violating a longstanding tradition that a shore facility never refuses water to any vessel. But just then the owner of a fifty-five foot flying-bridge monster in the next slip intervened by offering his hose to us and three words to the attendant, "Get lost, buddy!" Next, he drove Ginger into town to refill a propane tank. It takes all kinds. He was a rough sort of fellow who owned this $200,000 vessel. Turned out he'd built a ship's boiler-cleaning business based on the invention of some sort of unique rodding device.

On the way in to this marina we'd noticed some empty moorings so now we picked one up. Figured if marina staff came by for money, we'd just drop it and go anchor again. No one bothered us. Melanie was anxious to leave and since the airport was just three miles away, she hailed a cab and left us. Damn, we'll miss her.

Tomorrow we will head for Chesapeake Bay and its dozens of sheltered harbors. To get there, we must sail up the Delaware River for at least a day to reach the Chesapeake and Delaware Canal, a major, commercial waterway 14 miles long which flows from the Delaware River to the north end of 200-mile-long Chesapeake Bay. Actually it flows either way depending on ocean tides.

TUESDAY, NOV. 1: It was noon before we finally got off on our way to the Delaware. Leaving Cape May harbor one sails under the railroad bridge and through a short canal thus avoiding a venture into the mouth of the Delaware that can be so rough as to slow to a crawl any vessel smaller than a hundred tons. The canal dumped us into the river at an eastside bay where only a few yards to port there was a distinct line in the water more than a mile long; calm on our side but a heavy chop on the other. In about fifteen minutes this powerful shear petered out and we made our way NE to the main shipping channel for a four hour, slow, slog up-river against foul current. Checking the chart, it looked as if we could reach Back Creek on the Jersey shore before dark.

The sun was almost down when we turned out of the channel, and the shore was just too far away to see the small Back Creek entrance buoy but shortly I was able to spot it with the binocular. Once over the creek's threshold it immediately deepened to 25 feet so we motored quietly around four looping turns before it shallowed enough to make anchoring easy. Beautiful, lonely spot. We are surrounded by a huge marsh which extends in three directions, unbroken for miles. Not a tree or even a bush interrupts its surface; the top of this tawny grass is as flat as if cut with a shear. Way in the distance a thin, dark tree-line delineates the horizon. A gray, shuttered shack and a distant, wooden farm house are the only human creations in sight. We're snugged down in total solitude with the gentle clucking of a few ducks and shore birds settling in for the night. The setting sun adds more orange to the marsh grass that's so high I have to stand on deck to see over it.

In the morning, back to the big shipping channel we go, passing tall buoys every two miles. Finally, the C&D Canal entrance appears as an array of tall, open-steel towers with flashing, white lights and red and green traffic signals (which we, as an "inconsequential vessel," are allowed to ignore). The canal is at least a hundred yards across but, almost immediately we're surrounded by sheer earth walls that look much higher than the canal's width. No wonder it took nine years to dig back in 1869. Cars on the two bridges look like ants way above our heads. Beyond the midpoint of the canal is a little collection of shops which we decide to explore. The grocery was preparing to close for the winter but Ginger saw an item or two we needed, and in the liquor section were two quarts of Mount Gay Rum which she grabbed immediately when the proprietor quoted only $8.00 each.

There's not much to see as one emerges from the canal; Army munitions plants and other industry. But before long we turn into the Bohemia River's wide mouth and we're obviously in the Chesapeake. Forested shores rise gently from the water's edge interspersed with huge, immaculate, green lawns leading to white mansions in the middle distance. It was surprising to find so many coves occupied by marinas with docks or moorings covering every good anchoring spot. Found an acceptable place but not as secure as we'd like, and dropped our plow anchor. A quiet night however, made us very comfortable in this classic Eastern Shore scene. The weather is being kind to us in one way—no rain since we left the Vineyard!

THURSDAY, NOV. 3: Next stop is the Sassafras River; a bigger version of the Bohemia with many times more boats. At Fredericktown the big Skipjack Marina had a large store where we hoped to find a spare mantle for our indispensable Aladdin lamp but no luck. The store owner was very businesslike and the owners of the zillion boats were not around. Spoke to one other cruising couple in the store, intent on being on their way. We all feel winter closing in. With so many facilities closing down, and the weather so gray we're left with little chance for social contact and little inclination to hang around exploring ashore. Found enough space to anchor amongst dozens of moorings only because of our three and-a-half foot draft. No space at all for deeper keels.

FRIDAY, NOV. 4: An easy, five-hour sail down the Eastern Shore to Rockhall Harbor became complicated an hour before we got there. First, we had to round Swan Point to the east and deal with shallow Swan Point Bar which extends south for three miles with numerous three-foot spots, and then the big bay also full of shallows. The chart shows a 30-foot tower with a quick-flashing white light at the top, right in the middle of the bar in five feet of water and nearly a mile from shore, which turned out to be a range, a big help entering Rockhall. But next, our several charts of the area disagreed on the location of the channels and buoys leading in from the red and green on the ends of the two long breakwaters. We make it through the outside shallows and through the breakwaters into the harbor where, finally, we can see that the buoys have been removed from an "old" channel and replaced on a circuitous new route to port close to shore. More small buoys guide us around 180° before we can head to the marina in the starboard end of the harbor. The problem is that the entire harbor center has silted into no more than two feet deep. Having negotiated this roundabout mile we go aground in the mud turning to starboard at the last buoy approaching the marina. Backing off to try it again, this time hugging the buoy, we make it to the fuel dock. An old-timer type appears to take our lines. He's already seen our stern because he asks, "Tisbury? Martha's Vineyard?"

"Ah-yep," I say.

"'Do y' know Miles Carpenter?"

"Of course! He's a close friend," is my answer. With that, we'd made a friend who pointed out exactly where we should anchor without upsetting the marina owner and then drove Ginger two miles into town for ice. (Could be this is why people have bicycles on board?)

We nearly went aground again after leaving Rockhall the next morning on our way to Annapolis where we plan to spend several days. Sailing up the Severn a few hours later it was bitter cold and windy so we just anchored in the outer harbor and stayed below. Having been to the sailing center of Annapolis for boat shows years ago we knew we should anchor as close as allowed to the mouth of "City Dock," a long, narrow basin jammed with boats both working and pleasure. Its edges are occupied by businesses offering every imaginable supply for sailors including a truly world-class market/delicatessen athwart its end. With the outboard on our dinghy it was a mere ten minutes to all our needs the next day. Looked for a spare Aladdin mantle at Sadler's Hardware but no luck. The big, indoor market is a godsend of warmth.

The weather is very dreary, cold and windy. Not much above freezing each day and now Ginger's coming down with flu. There are many historic places to see here but it's not much fun walking around town when it's this cold. We wished to be much farther south; this is our third day here and we must push on. The forecast for tomorrow is warmer and light winds so I'm going to singlehand the four or five hours to St. Michael's while Ginger stays in her bunk.

The next morning I'm off by 9 AM. I'm now reading from *Lyla*'s log: "Wind calm. Sea condition flat, glassy cat's paws…Could see Bloody Point L' house six and a half miles away.…Black can WRI '3' not seen but two white buoys at this location." All small navigation aids, which would be floating nuns and cans in New England, are fixed marks on ten foot high pilings here. These will be the standard navigation marks from now on. Each pile has a large plywood triangle painted red for a nun, or a square painted green for a can plus a big number.

By 1:30 PM we'd sailed down the Miles River and into the creek at St. Michaels to tie up at the big Chesapeake Maritime Museum which consists of many historic or locally significant boats and their equipment displayed outside or in several big barns. Also there is a large boat shed with an extensive workshop for restoring boats and a Chesapeake-style, squatty lighthouse moved here from the middle of the bay. Ginger was feeling awful with fever so I searched out the admission-ticket kiosk to ask how I could find a doctor to come have a look. The nice lady there called her own doctor and talked him into making a boat-call! I think he thought it was a lark to get out of the office. He said Ginger was on the verge of pneumonia and should be ashore but she refused. I called Mel to come and help us until Ginger recovers and she joined us four days later—planes, bus, cab. She's amazing.

I visited my Aunt Catherine who lives just four blocks away. She invited us to use her guest room with Ginger sick but G. preferred the boat with meals close. Uncle Donnie seemed a bit remote (Donald Hiss, brother of Alger).

Bought a wick and spare mantle, at last, for our trusty Aladdin lamp in its swing-out bracket in a corner of the cabin sole. It not only keeps us comfortable but also dries out the boat. The latter would be a dreary place in prolonged cold weather without it. No sign of any leak or mildew anywhere in the boat! A little condensation runs down our big windows at times, but it's caught by the window frames. We have a DRY boat! That closed-cell, polyethylene foam really works.

Meanwhile the staff at the museum treated us royally. Partly this was because we had a "good-looking, proper and wholesome" boat and partly after they discovered I had boatbuilding and fiberglass skills. One day I helped them do a tricky "glass" job that they were a little hesitant to try. Luckily it was successful and from then on Chris McCready, the manager, gave me the run of the place including any materials I needed. I was even allowed to turn out a new special, bronze oarlock fitting for our dinghy on the metal lathe. A replacement would have had to be ordered from England so this was a huge favor. Everyone took the time to be exceptionally helpful to us in so many ways.

SUNDAY, NOV. 13: Departed early from the museum on a rather nice day. A little warmer, partial sun and eight to twelve knots of wind out of the north. Wouldn't you know, our course for the first six miles was due north. I very much wanted to tour up the Wye River where my grandfather had quite an estate in the early 1900's. My father often spoke of Wye Heights this and Wye Heights that. The unusual chandelier that hung over the dining table as I was growing up (and now dominates our own dining table) once hung in the circular staircase at Wye Heights. It would have been a five-mile trip to the Wye, then the winding Wye East to where it bends sharply north. The house was built on a cliff right there looking directly north up the river. Melanie, too young to have much interest in her great grandfather, was chomping at the bit to help us get south so I had to give in.

Onward to the Solomons as our nice breeze dropped to a glassy calm. One of the largest yachting centers in the Chesapeake, at the mouth of the Patuxent River, it is what appears to be an archipelago of three large creeks each with many scenic and sheltered anchoring spots. Solomons Island itself—which isn't quite an island—is inconsequential. Rather it is the adjacent confluence of no less than seven marinas and four boatyards along the squiggly shoreline which is called "the Solomons."

We pulled into Mill Creek, the prettiest of the three, explored up stream almost a mile looking at possible anchorages, turned around and came back to the second little cove where we just managed to edge off the channel for a peaceful night. Mel and Ginger snugged down in the latter's big bunk and giggled over the movie *Nine-to-Five* on our color TV. Ginger beginning to feel better. HOORAY!

While we have Mel, we'll push along as fast as possible; no exploring. Damn the cold weather and short days. We are missing a lot. Next year we should spend the month of October in the Chesapeake. The boat is finally properly stowed and we are very pleased with it. There's very little that we don't have and everything on board works! I've sailed on too many boats where this was not so. All the features I've built-in make handling and living free of difficulties. None of the many things we do routinely is awkward to do.

MONDAY, NOV. 14: We're off down the big, wide Chesapeake this morning to Deltaville, a fishing port on the west shore which several Vineyarders recommended. There's a light wind which became stronger as the day progressed. By late afternoon, eight hours later, the weather was stormy-looking and cold. The dredged channel into Fishing Bay began in shallow water way offshore, and because it was invisible, there was a range to keep us literally "on the straight and narrow." As we progressed into the outer bay, buoys, numbered from two to 57 (thus 56 buoys) outlined the channel beside winding shorelines for at least four miles. Sunset finds us rounding the long, skinny sand spit and heading into Deagles Marina which is all but closed down for the winter. We, the trimaran which has been in sight all day, and one other cruising boat are the only occupied boats around. Took some strong convincing before dock personnel were willing to put on their coats, turn on the pumps, go outside and get out the hoses to give us gas. Darkness fell quickly and with clanging halyards on deserted boats, the glaring, narrow beams from a few spot-lights on tall poles slicing through the cold wind, the marina seemed pretty desolate.

The girl in the office, just ready to head home, called Taylor's Restaurant which sent a car for us and we had an excellent dinner at their family-style establishment about three miles away. We were joined by the couple from the trimaran for a short time. Then back to the boat, fire up the Aladdin and snuggle down under a load of blankets. Just above freezing outside.

In the morning the wind was piping 15 to 30 knots in a gray overcast sky and we had to make the decision to go or stay. The trimaran is staying. Mel is eager to go so, grudgingly, I give in. First we tie a reef in the main and hank on the storm jib, stop it down to a lifeline stanchion and get underway. Out in the Chesapeake the seas built up quickly against the current, and were large and close together for the velocity of the wind. Blowing out of the SE it allowed us to ease sheets a little for a close reach. Before long the seas built up to more than eight feet. The helm became energetic to say the least, and demanding as I tried to ease her in to each wave. Straight down the back of a wave into the valley was best, where the next wave would block the wind and collapse the main. I'd then head up a bit and the main would fill with an fearful bang. The crests were probably a hundred feet apart but it seemed no more than 50! After nearly four hours of this, Mel and I taking turns at the helm, the boat fell off one particularly big wave and when the main filled, the reef cringle exploded right out of the sail. The swell must have been ten feet high; maybe fifteen. I was on the helm so Mel went forward to drop the sail and try to get it under control. I'd head up, possible only momentarily, and she'd get stop-cord around one part. I'd negotiate the next wave, head up and she'd get another part. The boat meanwhile was wallowing under engine and storm jib. Finally I managed to wrest the full-main cringle from the reef tied down on the boom and free the rest of the reef, sometimes steering with one foot or a knee. Mel hoists the main but the full sail is too much so she experiments with slacking the halyard a bit which helps. A gaff-rig sailor would call this akin to "scandalizing the main."

This works for almost an hour as the wind eases a bit, when BANG goes another cringle taking the whole corner of the sail with it. Now we go through the same drill again tying in a sloppy, double reef with a struggle. Our destination is Mobjack Bay. Its East River will have good shelter and I hope to visit a boat-builder friend who lives there. The Mobjack is full of fish weirs often over a mile long and made of long sapling trunks driven into the mud bottom and held together with steel cables. In the distance they look like a ragged picket fence. The chart shows a very long weir with the buoy we must use to enter Mobjack Bay right in the middle of it. It is illegal to build a weir which interferes with a navigation aid so Mel and I agree that there must be some sort of opening. As we draw near this weir it looks miles long to our right and to our left. But, we can't pick out the buoy. Having turned the corner toward Mobjack we are now on a broad reach running parallel with the waves at breakneck speed. *Still* no buoy, no opening. It would be a long way to turn and go around the weir's end and we'd be crashing into the waves again so we just keep going. We're getting terribly close. There's the buoy but no opening! I steer for the buoy thinking to just skin by it hoping not to be snared by a cable. At the last moment a tiny, offset opening appears and we shoot through unscathed. All in the day's work! Ginger's been below the whole time still weak from the flu. She hardly knows what she's missed!

New Point Comfort with its tall, slim, white lighthouse is well-named. Within a minute of rounding it we were in calm water and we covered rapidly the five miles to East River. In an hour we were on our way north, up the river, a very pretty and protected place. Clumps of nice houses with dense pine woods behind them and a number of boat building yards, all small but productive, several with big sixty-foot shrimpers under construction in wood. I wanted to put in to Put In Creek and call my friend in Mathews, Virginia, but Mel wouldn't hear of it. Nothing would do but to hurry on to Norfolk which, I had to admit was only logical. Once we've reached Norfolk she could call a cab and be at the airport in fifteen minutes. By 3 PM we'd anchored in a small cove sheltered by tall, thick pines, and settled in for a quiet night.

WEDNESDAY, NOV. 16 dawned partly sunny, a light wind and not so cold. Powered down river and out into Mobjack Bay as the wind rose. With two cringles blown out of the main we could sail only with a double reef so we thought to try the working jib which, to our surprise, gave perfect balance with the main on a close reach which was carried all the way south to Plum Tree Bar where the shore forced us to close-haul. The New Point Comfort Lighthouse stood out behind us in the sun for eighteen miles; this was a very fast, comfortable trip. Couldn't lay Wool Island so tacked back to the Naval Station off Old Point Comfort, then one last tack to the tip of Willoughby Spit and the marina nestled inside it.

It's a windy, lonely place, somewhat run down but it offered calm, well maintained slips and a good marine stockroom. There's no market nearby but Neptune's restaurant was only a short walk away. Moments after the boat was secured in a slip, Melanie, who's a pro in the food service industry, walked into the restaurant's back door and returned with a big bowl of hot, fresh shrimp she cadged from the cook. After drinks, a good shrimp dinner and music on the stereo, we were soon off to bed.

The next morning we lucked out with the torn sail. The marina manager recommended a small sail maker's shop less than a half mile away. The main was slipped off its tracks, bundled into the genoa's bag and carried to the Little Bay Canvass Shop where Melinda Wells did a first class job not only of replacing the two cringles with new ones but reinforcing the whole clew area of the sail with additional, feathered layers of Dacron sail cloth such that it would never blow out again.

We called a cab for Mel and she left for the Vineyard before noon. Her job was done as we will not be forced to go outside the Intracoastal before reaching Miami.

FRIDAY, NOV. 18: Next stop Norfolk, just around the corner. Hampton Roads, of course, is a huge harbor occupied by the U.S. Navy and every sort of commercial shipping. We were departing the harbor's east corner and heading into the Elizabeth River portion of Norfolk, and its central section which is ringed completely around by big marinas and about a mile of side-by-side slips for the Navy's biggest cruisers and carriers. Here also is the central Naval Hospital and Mile-Zero of the Intracoastal Waterway. Needless to say, it's a busy place with big tugs-and-tows, ferries, supply boats and launches maneuvering in every direction among the truly *big* ships.

The current was foul against us as we turned the corner and soon we were running in parallel with a big tow to starboard struggling against the current as much as we were. I sidled off to port as close as I dared under the sterns of the big ships in their slips and we began to pull ahead of the tug. A mile of this and we arrived at what is called Norfolk City Dock. A year ago a large and very nice, indoor mall had been built and the last part, yet to be finished, is this dock with a surrounding breakwater, or mole to fend off the constant wash and wakes of passing shipping. No sooner had we made fast at the bulkhead in front of the mall than a police officer approached. Of course I thought, uh-oh, but he was the jolliest of officers who announced that "your first night and your last night are free. More than that and you pay!"

Great! we intend to stay just one night. What a pleasant place the mall turned out to be: all the usual name-brand stores plus a large delicatessen and many specialty shops. It was so nice to find good French bread and fresh fish that we spent most of the day exploring and shopping.

SATURDAY, NOV. 19: Awoke to a nice day; some sun and not so cold. By 8 AM we were under way through the industrial portion of Norfolk. Big steel structures everywhere; warehouses or manufacturing buildings with tall stacks, huge docking facilities and cranes, great piles of coal and scrap metal, and two enormous, heavy bridges side by side. We call each one on the radio requesting an opening and finally the railroad bridge finds a moment between endless coal trains to open its ponderous self. The gates at each end close and it emits two long, shrill "toooots" that reverberate around the harbor as we and other vessels line up to go through, and the highway bridge beyond begins to open as well. Our little boat seems so miniscule under these monsters.

The waterway now begins to narrow to become the North Landing River and the industrial habitat is replaced by commercial/residential. In another hour we come to our next adventure, our first lock. It will raise us only about two feet but we've read in the *Waterway Guide* that everything must be done just right or the lock master will be uncooperative. Though we are circling slowly close to the lock's gate, we must first attract the lock master's attention so we give two toots of our horn, the standard signal for opening bridges. Nothing happens. We try calling on Channels 9 and 13. No answer. After about fifteen minutes I pull out the *Waterway Guide* to discover what I have missed.

Ahh. He opens only on two long and two short horn blasts. I blast the horn and immediately, the gates begin opening! Our fenders are already overboard so I edge the boat to the left wall below where the master is standing about ten feet above us and he swings down a long boathook on which I hang the eye-end of a mooring line which he drops over a bollard and walks forward to do the same for my bow line. I'd read that he won't accept the other end of a line which has no eye. Then we stand around on deck and wait. Eventually he receives a call from a bridge tender a quarter mile ahead that the latter has decided that traffic is light enough to allow him to open. Only then will the lock master free us from his lock. The whole process takes more than hour.

Another half hour takes us to our destination, Atlantic Yacht Basin, reputedly the best boat yard on the entire waterway. The owner of this large facility holds a contract for all dredging of the ICW in Virginia and North Carolina so it has the capability, both in equipment and personnel to service big dredges as well as yachts of all sizes. Its fuel and receiving area is a face dock right on the ICW. However, a hundred yards south, a deep creek leads off around to the west again to one of the most secure hurricane holes to be had. Its black water is absolutely still as it is surrounded on three sides by dense, seventy-foot pine trees and on the fourth by the yard's huge sheds which shelter, under roof, power boats up to seventy feet in length. Upon entering one of these sheds for the first time from the land side it is astonishing to face a 12-inch wide walkway over the dark water four feet below with nothing to grasp for balance but a single two-by-four handrail on one side running from one roof-supporting post to the next—and *they* are sixteen feet apart.

The yard has a good chandlery, excellent stock rooms, hull and engine repairs, cranes, travel-lifts and laundromat. For the cruising sailor it gets even better. A five-minute walk through the piney woods ends at a small downtown with supermarket, drugs, electronics, auto parts, bank, veterinarian, propane-refill, dry-goods and clothing stores, and two excellent restaurants. Finally, this is the place to leave one's boat for extended periods knowing that it will be safe and well looked after, a feature which we employed in the future.

Now, as we continued on our way, the landscape began to change. We crossed into North Carolina and the Pamlico Sound/ Cape Hatteras area where there were no more cities. Instead, we passed through great expanses of open marsh reminiscent of Back Creek in New Jersey interspersed with deep, narrow rivers, some downright impenetrable swamps, and small towns with the feeling of the old south in them.

Here and there we came across interesting spots, but we fetched up often in swampy places where we anchored only because darkness was falling, or in current-ridden creeks with long, gravel bars and edges of three-foot high, tangled, woody vegetation negotiable only by birds, snakes or insects. These are places where we spent nights at significant risk and where we graduated from anchoring 101 to advanced, two-anchor know-how.

Our New England/down-Maine training teaches: "Never anchor with two anchors off the bow. They will tangle for sure!" The truth is that this is both safe and effective. Yes, the rodes will wind around each other over several days but always just off the bow above the water, and so what. Yes, at times one rode will be riding aft along the hull and if you put the engine in gear, the rode can be sucked into and wound around the propeller, but you do this only once. You'll never let it happen again!

The next section of the Waterway is a rather boring, straight stretch of dug canal. A quick turn into a little side creek at Pungo Ferry for the night…and we were on our way by 8:30 in the morning hoping to make it across Albemarle Sound, but no. With wind from dead ahead at fifteen knots, enough to get some spray on the dodger, and *Lyla* thus slowed to four and a half knots, we didn't want to crash into big seas for hours crossing the Albemarle so we turned back north in the North River to Broad Creek. The beige ketch which had been just ahead of us, went on but they must have regretted the pounding they took in that wind.

Broad Creek branches off the west side of the river into a wild, desolate area with no sign of human presence. It's basically a swamp, but the creek itself is bordered by low, scrubby trees and bushes offering slightly more shelter than adjacent areas of open marsh grass. The whole aspect is gray—this is winter, after all—the sky is gray, the vegetation is all gray and the water, which is dark brown at any time of year appears gray too. I drop an anchor to hold *Lyla* in the mouth of the creek temporarily and put our inflatable dinghy in the water so that we can explore the depths. I row all over that creek and its little tributaries while Ginger mans the lead-line. It's all a good eight feet deep in the middle and five feet right to the banks. A smaller creek which doubles back on the main one is six feet at least. One could drop a hook out in the center of it and tie the stern to the big, round tree to starboard half way in with impunity. Though there are two other boats in here tonight, there's yet a spot where we drop our anchors, set them in well with the engine, hang the anchor light on the forestay and go below for the night.

MONDAY, NOV. 21: After washing a lot of sticky mud off the anchors and chains, we're under way by 8:45 AM. The wind is down to eight or ten knots, much less than yesterday, but, as we enter Albemarle Sound, we find waves occasionally as high as three feet; all out of proportion to the wind. *Lyla* pushes through them comfortably though we are slowed a bit. The Albemarle runs west-to-east and is more than 20 miles across. We are heading directly across it to the mouth of the Alligator River which runs south for ten miles before turning west for another five to Tuckahoe Point which we hope to make by late afternoon. After about twelve miles in this chop we can see the hills of the far shore with an open space which must be the two-mile mouth of the Alligator. I adjust our course slightly and aim at the west headland to compensate for current, checking our drift for several minutes before correcting to 220°, magnetic.

Another two hours pass before we can see the faint outline of the long bridge over the Alligator. It seems so skinny; just a thread high above that wide river. Finally, as we draw closer we can make out the tiny shapes of cars progressing across.

Sailing down the Alligator is boring and Tuckahoe is stark and bleak. Several decades ago, a change in the course of the river at that point flooded a forest of large trees which have now rotted away leaving only numerous tall trunks rising high above the tall grasses, their split tops pointing skyward.

WEDNESDAY, NOV. 23: Today we are looking forward to our destination, Whittaker Marina near Oriental, North Carolina, owned by the son of a Vineyard friend who has built a very nice facility; park-like grounds, swimming pool, attractive, well-stocked store. About 50 slips are nestled in a very secure pond deep in a dense, pine forest. We anchored out where there's five feet of water and room for at least four boats to swing.

On our way here, this morning, we had to leave the waterway because of a stuck bridge unable to open, and head east into the large, open part of Pamlico Sound where there are various navigation marks to be identified and sorted out before heading south around Maw Point into the Neuse River. In the log I see the following notes, "Hit all of these marks precisely until Neuse River mouth; then we seemed to be off a degree or two to port. Oriental is easy to spot and the Whittaker Channel mark is big. Be sure to stay right *on* the small range markers. The channel is very narrow and water on each side is only a foot deep." The comment about "off a degree or two" arose because it prompted me to check the compass for possible deviation while conditions were right to do so (i.e., there was no leeway from wind or current in the Neuse for a while). Pat West had swung our compass in Vineyard Haven and the old master had it right in its sweet-spot so we rarely suspect the compass for any anomaly; it always has to be something else. Nevertheless, "a degree or two off" compels me to check. It was right on. At times an adjuster doesn't achieve the sweet-spot or, under certain conditions, there may be no sweet-spot and the compass is more easily disturbed leaving skippers to suspect their compasses much of the time.

THURSDAY, NOV. 24: Woke to overcast skies and a weather report forecasting rain and wind later in the day, but as I look outside, the pond is glassy; no wind at all. What is the saying about "calm before a storm"?

It's about four miles across the Neuse here, and as we crossed it we expected to be able to see one of the buoys of a "wicket" (a red and green pair of buoys) at the entrance to Adams Creek, but no luck so we set a course of 130° which brings us close enough eventually, to spot them. They're small and hard to see.

Adams Creek is narrow and altogether lovely, displaying here and there ten-foot-high banks, occasional houses and a few isolated small industries all set neatly in the clear understory of a tall, pine forest which extends some sixteen miles to Beaufort and Moorehead City. We passed several side creeks that would offer nice anchorages for some future voyage. My plan is to spend a day or so at Beaufort which we'd been told has an interesting boat building industry, an excellent marine museum, and noteworthy sail boats at its waterfront.

Several miles north of the city the creek opened to a straight stream edged by long gravel bars and rushing current. It began to rain. Soon it was pouring! And it was time to watch for the turn-off into Gallant Channel with rain coming down so hard that I could hardly see. We made the turn and shortly entered a small pool behind the town of Beaufort where we had to size up many circumstances in a hurry. Several buoys appeared to lead to a commercial fishing pier. I didn't want to go there. Several other buoys appeared to be missing and the center of this hole was so shallow we could easily go aground. Making our way around to the far side, three sail boats on moorings materialized through the rain and several power boats were berthed at various docks close by. Finally we set our anchors near one of the moored boats, all without going aground. Whew! In turn, we each shed our foul-weather gear under the dodger and went below. After dinner the wind increased so I took several bearings with my hand-compass on lights ashore so that later I'd know if the anchors had dragged. I spent minutes watching just how *Lyla* and the moored boats were each swinging before I felt sure that we wouldn't collide if the wind continued to increase. Then off to bed.

I dozed fitfully, listening to every sound in this strange harbor, wondering whether the anchors would hold in an unknown bottom, and finally slept until about 1. AM Woke abruptly to the sound of the wind roaring and shaking the mast, wave-tops lashing against the hull. I got up to look out our large windows. The water surface was completely hidden by a foot-thick layer of white spume. The book says "Wind greater than seventy knots: spume covers the entire surface." Ginger was awake asking, "That's a hell of a lot of wind, isn't it?!"

"Sure is," I said looking aft out the companionway, "and we're dragging because we're closer to that boat docked behind us. We'll have to do *something*." I dove into the forward cabin where I sleep, opened the forepeak and began to pull out the 44-lb. storm anchor, its 15 feet of heavy chain and the 200 feet of line. Then all this heavy stuff had to be shoved up on deck through the forward hatch overhead, and quickly before the rain could soak my bunk.

I said to Ginger, "The boat has to be driven up into the wind to be even with the other two anchors so there's enough scope when we fall back to allow the anchor to hold. This may take the full power of the engine and will be very tricky as the boat will try to veer all over, risking getting one of the rodes caught in the prop so I'm going to do this, and you'll have to get the anchor ready to shove over. Be sure the rode won't foul when it runs out and then be damn sure you don't get caught in it as you heave that big anchor overboard when I shout out." (Ginger remembers that I added, "—and don't nick the rail's varnish!") She went up the companionway in her night gown, grabbed her foul-weather jacket and I followed, pulling on mine.

Out on deck the wind was roaring like a freight train, the rain stinging as it hit my face. I shouted "No time to put on a harness; hang on tight as you go forward and don't stand up!"

I started the engine. The boat was traveling from one side to the other in two big quarter-circles on the long anchor-rodes. It would pull back on both for a moment and then begin a slow swing to one side speeding up as it headed forward almost into the wind before tacking and falling back, then starting a swing to the other side. What I had to do was to interrupt one of those swings and try to drive the boat up, into the wind between the anchors where Ginger could drop the storm anchor. Trouble was that the wind blew the boat off its course, in spite of all my effort, and I had to fall back and try again. After two tries I made it and Ginger managed to get the 44 lb. anchor over instantly without it catching on the life-line, nor did the rode tangle as more than a hundred feet ran out in seconds.

Then it happened; one of the other rodes went slack, was washed aft along the hull and caught in the prop. I tried carefully to reverse it but no luck. The boat fell back and fetched up on that rode so now the boat was no longer anchored from the bow but nearly amidships, hanging almost broadside to all that wind, putting an enormous strain on the propeller shaft and the hull. Something had to be done. If I cut the rode I'd lose a valuable anchor. The rode, of course, was horizontal, deep below the water surface. I reached over the side with the boat-hook, hooked it but I couldn't budge it; it felt as stiff as a steel bar. I stood there thinking, noting that, for just a moment it would slacken. I hated to lose that anchor. Ginger said, "Why don't you tie the little fender-float on to it before you cut it?"

I replied that the rode will snap away so fast that the cut end would slip through any knot…but maybe if I cross-wrap the fender's thin line around the rode, there's a chance that it might hold. "Get the fender and I'll get some line to winch the rode up out of the water where we can get at it and we'll give it a try. Up it came and I reached out as far as I could, sort of braiding the thin line along it for almost two feet. My sheath-knife cut the rode instantly and it disappeared with a thunk! The boat swung back, bow to the wind, and we went to bed after toweling ourselves down.

By morning the wind was still too strong to do anything constructive, but off to starboard there was that little float bobbing in the waves! All day we bounced around too, waiting for the wind to calm. On the radio the Coast Guard said the winds had been over 85 for three hours, higher in the gusts. The remaining end of the cut rode was still around the winch so I pulled on it but it was fast to the prop. I started the engine and eased it very slowly into gear in reverse while I pulled….The rode unwound and came right off! What a relief! Now we have propulsion again and I'd not have to go diving in that cold, filthy, brown water.

SATURDAY, NOV. 26: The storm was over and life could get back to normal. The Danforth anchor was retrieved after considerable work; the mud on its chain showed it had been down in the bottom about three feet. Minutes later I had the big one up, mud all over the foredeck. We retrieved the little float and the plow-anchor's rode. I pulled the boat forward with it until it was straight up and down in the water but the plow didn't budge. Ginger drove the boat forward and from side to side while the rode was cleated—no luck. Finally I led the line aft from the bow, alongside the cabin trunk, put it around the winch and began to crank and wait. No luck. We ran the line across the cockpit to the other winch and Ginger got out the spare winch handle so we could crank on both winches. More waiting. Nothing! Except now the bow was pulled down nearly two feet closer to the water and the stern was high out of the water. I was afraid the stubby bowsprit would break.

Ginger said "Let's just leave it and go below for some lunch."

"Good idea!" A full half hour later there was a little "r-rap" sound on the deck over my head; the bar-tight anchor rode had gone slack. That powerful, steady pull must have drawn the anchor, ever so slowly, up out of the mud. I took up slack with the winch now, several times in about five minutes as it made its way free. I've never before or since experienced an anchor being buried so deeply.

Hoping to find Beaufort interesting we motored out of our hole, called the big railroad bridge to open for us and moved around to the town's front where many boats were stranded by the winds all along the adjacent banks. First, we tried to find gas. No gas. The fuel dock was blocked by huge menhaden ships and no one seemed to care. Resorted to using someone's private slip for a few hours while we walked into town looking for the museum, then for a market. Got neutral to bad vibes from everyone. The museum was not just closed but appeared permanently locked up, the market, tiny, expensive and dirty, the drugstore poor. The waterfront stores were tourist traps; most looked either brand new or faded and not "making it." Boat-building was either hidden away or not there at all. The boats anchored off the waterfront were the only interesting objects. In two hours we were ready to shove off.

Beaufort inlet, Moorhead City and the beginning of twenty-mile-long Bogue Sound form a complicated group of current-ridden passages among sandy, little islets. Nevertheless we took the opportunity to explore the famous inlet with the thought that on some future trip we might want to exit into the Atlantic here. No problem, the channel out to the Atlantic is wide and well marked although the buoys have to be moved after every storm as the sandbars shift constantly.

A few miles down Bogue Sound our chart showed a little channel leading west into an interesting-looking, forked creek called Peletier which might offer good shelter for the night. Once through the opening in the low bluff, it opened out into a very attractive, small, waterfront community of houses under tall trees which nearly met overhead. Plenty of room to anchor near a private dock whose owner soon came down to invite us to tie up—I'd just set two anchors, I was tired and not about to get them up and stowed—it was hard to refuse.

Two small boatyards occupied one end of the fork. The other was shallow so we explored it by dinghy discovering that it ended at a highway overpass. After hiding the dinghy under some bushes we walked less than a hundred yards to a first class shopping center where we had film developed in an hour and noted that about every sort of store we could need was here. We'll come back again! Slept well in this secure and pretty spot.

SUNDAY, NOV. 27: We're underway by 7 AM as we have a long way to go today. Bogue Sound turns out to be long and monotonous. A ten to thirty-foot high bank runs close to us on the west side and blocks our view of anything to starboard. To the east the sound is only a foot or three deep out of the channel but a mile or two wide. Marsh grass and bushes on the barrier beach holding back the Atlantic are pretty bleak. An occasional line of summer houses dot the horizon and mark the distant ocean shore.

The landscape continues like this, unbroken for nearly four hours before becoming tidal marshes with a profusion of winding, intertwined creeks feeding an occasional outlet (inlet?) to the Atlantic. Signs of human habitation are both scarce and primitive, and local names such as Sloop Point, and New Topsail Inlet seem derived from a time 150 years ago when this thirty miles of coast was infested by pirates who used their local knowledge of the shifting sand bars and tide-swept creeks to thwart pursuit by government schooners.

About the only reasonable anchorage in this stretch is one which the *Waterway Guide* mentions as an anchorage of convenience only. Just beyond Sloop Point we turned east into a narrow creek which quickly bent south again. At this second turn some small, beach-pines, crowding close to the shore, offer some shelter where the current had scoured the bank, and there we dropped our anchors on a bottom of clean, coarse gravel. They'll hold if the wind doesn't come on to blow. Several years later I came across a watercolor painting by Ray Ellis of this very spot. Evidently he, and his skipper, Walter Cronkite, also chose it for an overnight. We were tempted to dinghy ashore and hike the short distance over the sand dune to the Atlantic but chickened out when we realized that we'd have to tramp through someone's back yard.

MONDAY, NOV. 28: Wrightsville Beach. Our Vineyard friend, Miles Carpenter recommended this resort town, a favorite of nearby Wilmington, N.C. residents, and a marina right on the waterway, Carolina Yachts. We stopped there as it looked OK but found it not only charged 50 cents a foot but didn't sell gas, so we turned around and motored over to Seapath Marina which we had noticed as we went by.

Three blocks from the waterway, it became one of our favorites, fully protected from the wash of passing vessels, immaculate, friendly, excellent facilities, even a courtesy car to drive to the shopping center. We were glad that we'd saved our gas business for these people. Shortly we took off on a walk to explore the neighborhood and discovered Redix, a prize store for any boat person. In a collection of old, small, wooden buildings pushed together, with doorways leading from one to the next, Redix sells everything from many types of anchors to a fuel pump which we bought as a spare, to foul weather gear and fisherman's rubber boots, to sun tan lotion and insect repellents, to clothing such as beautiful, high quality wool and Dacron sweaters, slacks, shirts and hats for men and women, to hardware such as bolts, screws and marine fasteners, all at great prices. We were there so long that we had to hurry our walk over to Hieronymus Bosch's fish market, one of those which buys directly from local fishermen and wholesales to restaurants. Ginger bought fresh shrimp and oysters for two meals.

Back to the boat and then the shower rooms. There's a hot water shower on the boat but it *is* cramped, so occasionally when there's a nice, big one on shore, we go for it. On our way home in May or June we will stop here for sure to explore the shopping center and the town. We can see high-rise condos, a dozen streets of nice stores and a beautiful beach. Maybe we can also take a side trip up the Cape Fear River to the city of Wilmington.

The weather has been warmer for a week now but obviously it won't last so we must push on. Sunny today but not much above 45°. The countryside in this area is much more attractive than Bogue Sound; less raw-looking—both trees and shrubs more luxuriant. Poked into Carolina Beach for the night. It's a pleasant-looking beach community whose ocean shore is crowded with summer houses which back up to a long, narrow, and surprisingly deep harbor blocked at one end by towering, ancient sand dunes which look to be more than a hundred feet high. The big Loran tower can be seen for many miles and is currently one of only five on the whole Atlantic coast. We backtracked out in the morning to go right through the dunes in Snow's Cut which empties into the Cape Fear River system, a broad estuary of marshes, sand banks and strong currents. The passage through the cut is spectacular; it looked deeper than any interstate highway cut I have ever seen—amazing that it is all white sand. The river is big and powerful, worthy of its name, three to four miles wide at this point. And though the five-mile trip down the river was uneventful, we were busy threading our way through a maze of channels and coping with the current even though we had timed it to be fair. I've put a note in the log that an attempt to sail this stretch against the current would add at least another hour.

It was evening when we reached the junction where Little River Inlet joins the ICW. Just north of this confluence is a pretty, and therefore popular little cove nestled among high trees which provide good shelter. As many as six boats could anchor in six-foot depths. Since we were number four to arrive we had to place our hooks carefully so as not to bother anyone else. "Bother" is the operating word here. A skipper who is already settled in will almost invariably stick his head out of his companionway looking askance if you should intrude into any part of what he thinks of as his surrounding water where you might run in to him during the night as current or wind or both change.

The wind quieted as the sun set so we pulled our dinghy up to the stern and hopped in to row around a bit for exercise and to explore the other boats. Struck up a conversation with the skipper of the boat nearest us and soon his wife appeared from below. We hit it off immediately and they invited us aboard for a drink. David and Zora Aiken. We laid plans to meet again, possibly, in other anchorages as we each work south. They have been living aboard *Zorka* for six years; he paints watercolors in their forward cabin while she writes for various boating magazines in the aft cabin and thus they are able to continue cruising year-round.

FRIDAY, DEC. 2: Georgetown, South Carolina, is really a small city big enough to support a steel mill. We arrived here after a pleasant sail down the Wacamaw River. Broad and beautiful, bordered on each side with cypress and pines, it is deep to the banks so we could put aside the charts which for weeks we've had to refer to every few minutes. Georgetown has very little tidal change throughout the day so we made fast to a dock on pilings for a change. As we walked past several other boats, there was *Ayuthia*, a 52-foot ketch and her owner, an ex-boyfriend of our daughter's. He and his wife had left Vineyard Haven nearly a month before we did. A shout down the companionway brought Tom and Fala up from below and exclamations flew back and forth. He'd earlier caught some fish so we were all soon below having lunch and comparing experiences. They are headed for the Abacos in the northern Bahamas while we plan to sail around to Florida's west coast so we probably won't meet again.

The next day we hoped to make Charleston but were just too late to make the Ben Sawyer bridge before it stays closed through the rush hour, so we turned off into Inlet Creek. Not a pretty place but it's deep and quiet with high banks cut into the marshes. It's also narrow and current-ridden as the tide flows in and out of the nearby inlet changing height more than five feet.

After setting anchors up and downstream I experienced a phenomenon I'd been told about but could hardly believe. The boat had settled with *its stern instead of its bow* to the wind in a fresh breeze which, of course, seems not only impossible but discomfiting as it blows down the companionway among other problems. I walked forward to find out what was going on.

The bow *appeared* to be breasting forward pulling on both rodes, each of which was stretched aft along the hull as if the boat was moving forward but directly down wind; a very strange feeling. It was the current running against the wind, of course, and stronger than the wind but not much, since the inactive rode was evidently making a U-turn under water where I couldn't see it and pulling gently against its anchor which actually was up stream. All I could do was close the companionway and turn the ventilators around.

Just then another boat turned in which turned out to be *Zorka*. It was our turn to have the Aikens aboard and Ginger did dinner in style. We were fascinated with their stories of life aboard with no home anywhere ashore. Every day, live-aboards must cope with the fact that modern life in the U.S.A. is built upon assumptions that everyone has a car, a house, a telephone number, a permanent address, but we don't. (Well, the Joneses don't fully qualify but we come close.)

This is a good time to write about anchoring; it's a little bit of art and a lot of practice. Every morning we pull the anchors up and every evening we put them down. If they're not put down right we could have a hell of a night. The very survival of the boat depends on successful anchoring. By now we're getting pretty good at it and we've learned that only with two anchors do we feel secure. Right now, for instance, on one anchor the boat would be wandering erratically over a large part of this creek obeying the varying forces of wind and tide. And later, when we'd be asleep and the tide reverses direction, the boat would swing around traveling nearly 200 feet to pull in the opposite direction against that anchor and possibly tear it loose. With two anchors, neither anchor will have to turn, and as the tide reverses, the boat will travel perhaps fifteen feet.

The stowage of anchors and rodes (lines and chain) is one of the most visible differences between long-term and weekend cruising boats. On a live-aboard's foredeck there will always be at least two anchors—not stowed below. And an inefficient system for handling all this stuff twice a day before long becomes a real bore. Easy-over and easy-retrieval begins with a strong, stubby bowsprit fitted with a heavy-duty roller. Each anchor with its heavy chain is stowed ready to run immediately with a yank on a quick-release knot while, at the same time, the stowage of an attached, big, heavy, somewhat-stiff hank of line must be coiled so neatly that it will always run freely even after heavy seas, coming over the bow, have tried to wash it about.

The bitter end of one rode must be available to unwind the twisting that occurs around the other rode after several days. The rode on our No. 1 anchor, a CQR plow, is 180 feet long plus 12 feet of heavy chain, totaling enough to pay out when setting a second anchor. 120 feet plus chain is enough for the 22 lb. Danforth. Both rodes have scope markings every 20 feet. One, two, three and four red bands at 20, 40, 60, 80 feet; then a double band, red and black, at 100 feet, and the same for black bands at 120, 140, 160 feet. We like to pay out a scope of at least four times the water depth, often five. There are three spare rodes on board, enough to serve any extraordinary needs I can imagine.

SUNDAY, DEC. 4: At about 10:30 we entered Charleston Harbor, a big body of water which forms the mouth of the Ashley and Cooper Rivers. The city is on a peninsula between them which we had to sail around to get to the far side with its two marinas. A rather nasty chop slowed us down for nearly two and a half hours. One look at the City Marina told us we didn't want to go in there; it's surrounded by a high concrete wall closing off all view outside of it. The Ashley is smaller, quite adequate and friendly.

Charleston is, of course, a place to do some sightseeing. We took a trolley-bus through the historic district, picked up some brochures and continued to the other side of town to a very nice supermarket. Here again we needed a pair of bicycles.

The next morning we visited two houses on the historic list, interesting outside but rather shabby inside. A long walk through this area was fun and good to shake our legs for a change. Weather partly sunny and only a bit chilly. We are hardened to the cold now. Nice city.

The Waterway leaves the broad Charleston Harbor via Wappoo Creek, a side stream where we passed several nice, modern houses in the Charleston suburbs before we were back in the marshes again. Clumps of trees here and there alongside miles of twisting rivers, deep to their banks. And everywhere how the wind did blow! Thirty knots with gusts to thirty-five or forty kicked up a four to five foot chop in the Wadmalaw. The Ashpoo River was a short, wild ride down wind. But then it was a long thrash, up wind in the Coosaw. Nor is the area attractive, so we were glad to reach Beaufort (Bee-u-fort) for a quick overnight stop before continuing on across Port Royal Sound to Hilton Head where we'll visit Ginger's cousin, Sallie Doughty. After dinner I sat down to write to my father whom we keep somewhat informed of our whereabouts. He is fond of doggerel and the sounds of words so I couldn't resist writing this:

> Greetings to you from the Toogoodoo
> Where a gale stopped us short of the wild Ashpoo.
> That wind made a mess of the Wadmalaw
> As we drove hard into its howling maw.
> It seemed to say, just you wait,
> Till you reach that bend in the old Coosaw.

If you think I made up all these names,
Take out your atlas and look up same.
You'll also discover just where we are.
Hilton Head is not very far.
In fact its only another day's sail.
We'll be there tomorrow to pick up our mail.

THURSDAY, DEC. 8: Our approach to Hilton Head was somewhat tedious as we had to sail past two thirds of the island in Calibogue Sound (pronounced Calibeaugey) to get to the mouth of Broad Creek and its very long sand bar running parallel to our course. Eventually we made the u-turn around the end of it and backtracked for two miles up this creek—which nearly cuts Hilton Head in half—in order to reach Palmetto Bay Marina which Sallie had informed us was the best.

The marina looked attractive with extensive floating docks and many boats in slips protruding out from shore almost to mid-river, but anchoring is our preference so we cruised on up stream a bit where we noticed a big schooner and a ketch anchored in line along the shore. "Ah!" Ginger said. "There's just enough space between them where we can slip right in." And slip in we did with a mud bank close on one side, and passing river traffic of work boats, fishermen and pleasure craft on the other. The owners of these vessels later remarked how we placed our anchors up and down stream so that their boats would not run far over them, and that *Lyla* settled exactly centered between them. I was pleased because often, when an "interloping" vessel inserts itself between "regulars," there's some grumpiness. Turned out that they are long-term residents with jobs in town.

It was a convenient three-minute row into a slip set aside for dinghies, but so much dead bulrush from the adjacent marsh piled up in the slip on the ebb that one had to push it all away with an oar for several minutes before being able to disembark. The marina has a small boat yard with a travel lift, and it services about thirty condos in a five story building. Dinner in the restaurant enabled us to meet some of the regulars including the schooner owners.

The next morning Sallie picked us up for a tour of the island and of her big, very nice gift shop in the leading hotel of this posh island. The latter is only about 8 miles long but it is loaded with high-class shopping centers, international boutiques, two big resort hotels, several championship golf courses and tennis courts. Of course it has fine, long beaches and first rate deep sea fishing too. What a place! Every kind of store one can think of. It wouldn't take long, I suspect, before it all would become a little much.

MONDAY, DEC. 12: We left Hilton Head this morning and we've been in one deep creek after another, all day, making our way through the enormous, spectacular expanse of what poet, Sidney Lanier was moved to describe as, "The length, and the breadth and the sweep of the Marshes of Glynn." Miles and miles of flat, yellow, marsh grass reaching to a far horizon delineated as a thin, dark-green tree line. Wow!

Tuesday we passed Jekyll Island famous for its Rockefeller and Vanderbilt mansions built in the 1880's. Scampi's nice-looking restaurant is right on the dock. Tie up and walk 20 steps down the pier to its door. A definite stop on our way home.

About noon we passed through the lift bridge to St. Simon's Island and a new marina on the west shore next to a resort-style shopping center under construction. Another definite stop on our return trip.

No decent anchorage exists in the next stretch of the ICW so about 4:30 we turned into Crooked River where the only shelter is an eight foot high gravel bank. Not a single tree or so much as a big bush for miles. I worked our anchors in hard with reverse engine and they seemed to hold. We're both uneasy in this bleak, lonely place but it will have to do. No sooner had we gone below for our evening cocktail than we heard a motorboat approaching. It slowed slightly then continued on—an open cockpit, but roofed-over launch with four or five of the toughest-looking young guys imaginable. What did they have in mind? Were they just on their way home from work? What would we do if they came back later? Well...after we'd finished our drinks it was getting dark and the thought of pulling up anchors and finding another spot seemed almost as risky so we had a quick dinner, snuffed out our lamps and went to bed. We heard not another boat all night.

WEDNESDAY, DEC. 14: We have arrived in Florida! Somehow this felt like some kind of a goal reached. We tied up at the long, face dock at Fernandina Beach. It's one, long wooden bulwark some 15 feet high with only slippery, iron-rung ladders to climb up. The tidal range here is about seven feet so I guess the remainder is to fend off storm surges. The other problem is what comes out of the high stacks of a paper mill a half mile away. The smell is familiar but here the "essence-of-paper-mill" is overpowering. In the morning one's boat is littered with what looks like inch-long black twigs. I tried to pick one up but it just smeared into the deck like so much grease. It was a week before we cleaned off the last one.

The landscape has changed. Gravel-washed banks and rushing currents have been replaced by oyster beds, fields of low palmettos, palm trees of course, and what the nautical chart calls "spoil banks." Much of most of Florida's rivers is so shallow that channels must be dredged. Years ago the dredges left acre-sized piles of sandy mud in the shallows alongside their work, and subsequently mangroves and sizeable trees sprouted and flourished to create pretty little islands. At first we thought what nice places they were to anchor but, all too often, the water leading to them was only a foot or so deep.

Now we encountered a small city or a town every few miles; it felt rather good to return to civilization. Enough of swampy marshes in the middle of nowhere. But then there were places like Jacksonville Beach where we felt like a big hawk being picked on by a bunch of crows—little outboards speeding around everywhere, and marinas which welcomed only big sport-fishermen with big tuna-towers and bigger fuel tanks.

Eventually, as the Tolomato River opened out before us, we came to the old, Spanish city of St. Augustine. A large, open bay off its waterfront provided an inviting anchorage and the city dock offered all the necessary services and even some rare pleasures. We needed kerosene for our lamps, ice and a few groceries. Spent a leisurely day sight-seeing, starting with a ride around town in a horse and buggy. The old, star-shaped, Spanish fort has been nicely restored and we learned some new details about canons weighing as much as two tons.

SATURDAY, DEC. 17: Stopped at Marineland to see their famous dolphin show. These animals certainly act nearly as humans, full of fun and affection for their trainers. Marineland's marina is tiny and had no room for us so, heeding Miles Carpenter's advice, we turned into a straight little creek at ICW mile 809. Only a few hundred yards long it ended at the towering, gray silos of a closed cement plant. High banks offered shelter and there was good holding and plenty of room for three other boats which came in after us.

This stretch of the ICW is not very attractive, just low, flat bushes and grass, some trees in the distance, scattered houses, small industries, a few small marinas up narrow, dredged channels through very thin water to the east. A single buoy or a stake or two, at the most, to guide one to them.

The next day we'd planned to stop in Daytona for gas. It was absolutely pouring rain as we went through the first of Daytona's four bridges across the waterway and just as the second was closing behind us the engine changed its note. "Huh?" I said to myself looking at the water temp gage. "GeeZUS, 230°!" Quickly I turned around and peered over the stern: no water coming out of the exhaust. Shut her down, NOW!

So here we are with another bridge coming up, other boat traffic behind us in the channel and poor visibility in the rain. As I steer out of the channel and we coast to a stop, the up-coming bridge tender calls on the radio, "Sailboat approaching Main Street Bridge. Do you wish an opening?"

"Aaah, Main Street. This is sailing vessel *Lyla*. I have engine trouble. Will anchor here and try to fix it, over."

Ginger takes the helm and watches traffic as I pull on a foul weather jacket and go forward to drop the plow anchor. (I *had* been sitting sans jacket, nice and dry under the dodger). Luckily the wind drifts us backward as I slowly pay out line to gain enough scope to set the anchor. Now, I'll have to get down into our starboard, cockpit seat locker to get at the pump. As soon as I open the seat-hatch the rain pours in, wetting three big bags of sails. No matter, I heave them out, grab a flashlight and several tools and climb in shutting the seat hatch on top of me. In five minutes I have the pump off and apart. Sure enough the rubber impeller has destroyed itself. Ginger hands me a spare impeller and in another few minutes it's all back together. Ginger starts the engine as I watch over the stern…Ah, lots of water. Anchor up and stowed, we call the bridge tender and we are off to the marina for gas.

In another two hours we pass New Smyrna Beach which looked much nicer than Daytona—a note in the log for our next trip. Then Mosquito Lagoon, a twenty-mile long, elliptical body of water no more than three feet deep anywhere except in the dredged channel down its middle. Darkness caught us at about sixteen miles whereupon we poked our bow into the mud alongside the channel half a dozen times before we penetrated the mud bank far enough to be out of the way of any passing boats for the night.

The lagoon's southern end is the closest place from which to watch a Canaveral rocket launch, but our timing, this morning, was not right to witness one. Just short of the lagoon's end is a thin strip of land, not much more than a sand bar separating Mosquito from the Indian River. In early American history men used to haul boats across it to gain water-access to most of the rest of Florida. Now, the bar is wider and crossed by the Haulover Canal. Saw two flocks of white pelicans, slightly bigger than brown ones and quite rare.

This morning we hope to sail about 40 miles to *The Dragon* and round up into the Banana River to visit my old friend Tom Downey. Long, skinny Merritt Island—which separates the Indian River from the Banana River—ends with a needle-like point on which is a landmark known to every ICW mariner: a huge, lifelike, concrete dragon at least 75 feet long. If one sails close by, an empty egg shell and two baby dragons perhaps ten feet long appear.

About ten years ago Tom pulled up stakes in Connecticut and sailed his 32-foot Colin Archer ketch to Merritt Island. First, he and wife, Peg, built a boathouse to live in while he built an attractive house next to it and, finally, a substantial dock. When we arrived, there was ample space for both our boats.

The next morning, as we were having breakfast, Ginger said, "Look," pointing out the window toward the boat-house. There, standing on the railing, not twenty feet away, was a great blue heron as tall as the railing.

Unfortunately we have brought the cold weather with us. Our outside thermometer read 28° and it remained almost that cold for the next three days. The banana trees all turned brown and Florida lost most of its orange crop. We were able to keep our boat warmer than Tom could keep his house. It was bitter out in the wind. Our search for warm weather has taken us more than 1200 miles from Martha's Vineyard and we have yet to find any of it.

TUESDAY, JAN. 3, 1984: The Indian River is a significant body of water 100 nautical miles long and a mile or so wide. Only in a few places is it as wide as two miles. It *was* also not much deeper than adjacent Mosquito Lagoon but, since man got to work on it, the mosquitoes are gone and a wide, ten-foot-deep channel has been dredged from end to end leaving pretty little spoil islands by the dozen. The west bank tends to be a little higher than the east shore which is the marshy edge of narrow, but full-length barrier-beach islands. Here, and on the mainland west of the river, is a succession of small towns and a few big cities which have built nice harbors, each with a marina or two, while leaving room in between for orange and grapefruit groves beside which we could "anchor out."

Someone had said, "Don't miss a stop at the Citrus Dock." So we turned off at the appropriate channel marker and found ourselves surrounded by an orange grove. The drill is to anchor opposite the orchard's store and show up in the morning for free juice—only the oranges weren't ripe yet so, of course, the store didn't open. Oh well! What could be nicer than to anchor in an orange grove? The weather has turned almost warm; at least warm enough to do some varnishing which the toe-rails so badly need. Spent the afternoon washing off salt with fresh water and sanding.

WEDNESDAY, JAN. 4: Sailed all morning and arrived at Vero Beach after lunch. The river narrowed here because there were several adjacent creeks hidden behind small oaks and pines. Just before the bridge we pulled into one of these creeks to reach the municipal dock situated beside a very nice, shady park, trees and mangroves all around us.

Room for about six boats opposite the dock and more up stream. We paid a dollar to fill our water tanks with the best water we'd tasted for weeks (the tanks hold 74 gallons). Anchoring is free and the attendant pointed out a small adjacent creek up which he said was a special, low float where we could safely leave our dinghy and go ashore exploring. This is the exclusive, barrier-beach side of Vero Beach; high-rise condos and some nice stores including one with fine Spanish and Italian tiles of which we bought a bag-full.

Then we *had* to wander through the Driftwood Inn. It was built during the early thirties by the parents of Ginger's college roommate. At first it was almost entirely built of driftwood but now it has been upgraded to a first rate establishment without losing its atmosphere. Fun to see.

THURSDAY, JAN. 5 & 6: Another sunny day is most welcome as we complete our trip to the end of the Indian River where it joins with the Saint Lucie River and the latter's inlet to the Atlantic. We have slipped through the narrow entrance to Manatee Pocket, a charming, small body of water surrounded by nice waterfront houses, a boat yard, a marina, a few stores within walking distance and a good friend who was the proud owner of Swiftsure No. 1.

In 1959 the Horrocks had fallen in love with the Swiftsure when it was first introduced at the New York Boat Show. Then and there Bill bought the vessel on display. The four of us can talk boats endlessly. Spent an extra day here enjoying these friends and exploring this pretty area with them.

Manatee Pocket is not the only attractive spot in the area. The whole Saint Lucie River, its north and south forks and the city of Stuart are the nicest parts of Florida we have seen so far. The south fork also leads to Lake Okeechobee and the Caloosahatchee River which cuts right across central Florida to Fort Myers on the west coast, and this is where we are headed next.

Too much of what we have seen of Florida suffers from uncontrolled growth. Only here and there have we come upon a good looking house or pretty landscaping. The sandy, white, limestone soil seems to offer too little sustenance to support soft green grass or plants. That which does manage to flourish is hard and spiky, even the grass is coarse and patchy. Strip development predominates. Looking back in the log as I write this, the previous seven pages contain virtually nothing but navigational notes. Except for Vero Beach and St Augustine, there are few places we'd come back to.

The bird life, however, continues to be entertaining every day as we meander along the waterway at five or six knots, a speed which allows so much opportunity to take in everything. The call of a common crow differs distinctly over long distances; here in Florida it raucously pronounces our human expression, "aw-oh, aw-oh."

Of course shore birds abound. herring gulls are always somewhere in view and small flocks of willets struggle to be airborne, flapping out of our way uttering their rapid whit-whit whew—whit-whit whew—whit-whit whew. Great blue herons, little blue herons, greater yellowlegs, cattle and snowy egrets work the shores. Sandpipers scuttle from our small wake as it reaches shore and on a low bush there's an occasional kingfisher. Coots and mallards busily feed on whatever is just below the surface. Cormorants perch-on-buoys, anhingas, grackles and redwing blackbirds in the trees. A sharp eye will spot a green heron or a limpkin pretending not to be seen along the shore. Ducks are surprisingly rare except for the occasional mallard pair, but in the evening, especially in the Carolinas, just after we have anchored for the night, the Canada geese sometimes swarm in and surround us. The noise from several hundred of them is deafening but by dark they calm down and shut up so we can all sleep.

The once threatened osprey has made a great comeback by using the tops of the tall navigation pilings to build nests, dozens and dozens of them wherein we often see a little head sticking up as we go by. Always there's a turkey vulture somewhere overhead, or perhaps a red-tail, or a marsh hawk, or terns swooping, or skimmers speeding with their red bills just touching the water, or the precision flyers, the pelicans. In small groups, perfectly in line, they'll fly half a mile, a few inches above the wave-tops without ever touching a wing-tip. Though we spend four to eight hours every day in the cockpit, there has never been a moment of boredom. This cruising is a full-time job!

MONDAY, JAN. 9: We left Manatee Pocket this morning and headed up the St. Lucie to enter its south fork. After passing several nifty houses, in about five miles the river narrowed to a canal. Ginger spotted an alligator on the bank; it must have been ten feet long. Weak sun and cool—almost no wind. Miles Carpenter has told us to stop at the tiny marina in Indiantown and look up Ed Mickey about joining the Indiantown Yacht Club. Like the marina, this tiny organization quietly exists solely to provide, for miniscule fees, reciprocal privileges with most eastern yacht clubs; a real perk for serious cruisers such as ourselves.

We went right by the opening in the high bank without seeing it and had to turn around in order to squeeze through into the marina's lilliputian pond. Surprisingly there are about twenty slips. At the fuel bulkhead the manager pointed and said, "Take the space over by the alligator." I headed in that direction looking for that name on a vessel next to the open space. Then we saw what he meant; an eight foot alligator lying on the float! At first, it didn't move at all as we sidled up to within three feet of it but finally, with a great show of annoyance, it flopped off the other side into the water and disappeared.

The only pretty part of Indiantown is the marina. The rest is all open, brown farm country with a majority of Native American workers. There's a market, one restaurant, and a farm machinery dealer about a mile away, and that's it. Also, unfortunately, Ed was in New York.

Tuesday morning, after a 9:30 start we had the railroad bridge at Port Mayaca in sight before noon. It's a heavy, rusty old lift-bridge 49 feet in the air between the two towers. The closer we came to it the lower it looked. I began to worry that it might not be all the way up! Our mast is 44'-11". Well, we *did* clear under it—and immediately afterward we came to the lock leading to Lake Okeechobee.

Here are some notes from our log book (info for next year's trip):

> Port Mayaca Lock was entered on flashing green, after a flashing red which showed until gates fully open. Lifted about three feet and entered lake. Nothing ahead but a horizon-line. Course 222½°. Picked up mid-channel, red day-mark right on 222½°. Out of sight of land 360° for over an hour, 3:40 PM. Two platforms appeared at Rocky Reef, 6° off stbd bow and a red mark on port slightly thereafter. L-hand platform turned out to be green mark #7 but

sign board missing—no color visible. Both platforms hung with a lot of stuff; looked like fish-traps. #14 is a big slotted triangle on 4 legs about 16' to 18' high. Turn here. 1 mile. Beginning of Clewiston Channel is a concrete pill-box (20' diameter) which looks 18' high. The ICW is seaward of lock; confusing.

Tall, casuarina trees line both banks forming a narrow arboreal canyon. Beyond them, along the lakeside, are acres of high grass. We followed this waterway north about a mile, set an anchor at the edge of the channel, dropped back in south wind and tied the stern to a melaleuca tree in ten feet of water. Some snags and weed in a sticky mud bottom so I buoyed the anchor. Great shelter in the shadow of these huge trees. Local fishermen running by in fast outboards were disturbing the quiet, but not a problem as they all suddenly disappeared just before dark. Beautiful place probably comfortable in any weather. Many mosquitoes, however.

The next morning we continued along the tree-lined waterway as it followed the edge of Okeechobee for nearly seven miles to the Moore Haven lock where we dropped back from the three feet we gained at Port Mayaca. Now we are in the Caloosahatchee River which flows for nearly 60 miles all the way across Florida. Actually, it doesn't flow because there are locks at each end plus two near its middle, so for a change, we don't have to give a thought to tides or current. The land is very flat, open and Texas-like—trees only along the river—I never knew that Florida has cattle country.

The river, never wider than about 150 yards, used to flow in an unending series of winding loops before the Corps of Engineers cut a ten-foot-deep channel straight through the middle of them. This left many little ox-bow half-loops, some with a clump or two of small trees, nice little private anchorages for one boat each. We are charmed; no waves, no wakes, no currents plus shade and shelter from the wind. Also, if we were to stay longer, the fresh water would kill the slime, grass and any barnacle which might have grown on our hull. It would all slough off and we'd gain a knot of speed.

Off again in the morning at 9 AM. More river, straight through the ox-bows but now more orange groves and other trees; the Texas-look is gone, the landscape more inviting. We made many miles yesterday so we'll make Fort Myers soon after lunch.

Fort Myers Marina is large and walled off from the river with concrete walls. In an hour we'd filled our water tanks and taken on 17 gallons of fuel. The staff seemed as uninviting as the walls, so after checking out the marine supply store we departed to explore further. Just beyond the second bridge the chart indicated depths off the port side of the channel that may have been an old side-channel leading past a small pier at the back of a Ramada Inn. We sounded our way over to it, found no less than five feet and, the forecast being for light winds, anchored about 30 yards off the bulkheaded shore right down town. We dinghied over to the Ramada's dock, encountering no one to ask about leaving the dinghy or when the pier gate might be locked (?!). Then we kind of snuck through the Ramada lobby, nobody accosting us or paying any attention, so we went on through to the street discovering a big shopping center almost across the street from us and the Thomas Edison Home three blocks down.

If you are ever in this vicinity, don't miss this museum. Edison's large lab looks exactly as he might have left it one afternoon a hundred years ago. The atmosphere of the entire house is light and airy. Original light bulbs, with their little spike tops, line the walls in sconces. They glow dimly as I'm sure the voltage is turned way down to make them last. There's interesting equipment everywhere, most of it handmade in his machine shop. His helpers learned fairly quickly how to make a single carbon filament which would last for a few weeks but they experimented for more than a year before discovering an alloy which could be manufactured in quantity and last as long as a year.

Outside in the extensive garden is one of the biggest ficus trees in the world. Its canopy must be forty yards in diameter. Back through the Ramada to find the pier gate still unlocked. Whew! Ginger had stopped at the front desk to ask about the pier. The clerk seemed to know nothing about it so it seems that we could make use of this convenient, free anchorage again.

FRIDAY, JAN. 13: The Caloosahatchee widens out at its junction with San Carlos Bay, into a profusion of small islands, points of land, sand bars and several channels all hemmed in by the mainland on the east and the big islands of Sanibel and Pine Island to the west. Just as we were negotiating this area we saw a familiar looking sailboat coming toward us. It was Ted and Holly Thomas in their Swiftsure *Escapade* (the boat that had introduced us to the class). Great exclamations shouted across wind and water between boats as we passed. He is heading for the same little cove as we, Shell Point. In a few minutes both boats made it over the cove's shallow threshold—it was nearly high tide. We turned left and anchored close to shore in five feet. Ted turned right, toward the middle of the cove, and promptly went aground in soft mud. Oh well, par for the course.

The cove is surrounded by twenty-foot high mangroves which provide a cozy feeling of shelter. The Thomases dinghied over to *Lyla* and we all had drinks and dinner below. It was ten before we'd caught up on each other's adventures, and by then, the dozens of herons that had been arguing loudly over who would settle where in the tops of the mangroves had quieted down. A north-east wind came up later and blew fairly hard till sunrise—we could hear it but the cove remained calm.

Ted was up early, started off and ran aground again momentarily. We were ready soon after as we are scheduled to meet Ginger's sister and brother-in-law in Sarasota two day's sail from here. They're scheduled to arrive by air from California and they would be stranded in a city strange to them if we were not there waiting.

After an hour threading through various channels among small wooded islands we entered wide and long Pine Island Sound (four miles by sixteen miles), which rates as one of the prettiest areas in this part of Florida. Several of its many islands are well-known—Captiva and Useppa especially. We want to come back here to explore nice-looking places and intriguing, possible anchorages. The water is gray-blue with turquoise shallows and the dozens of islands are heavily wooded with a scattering of houses, quite hidden, on the larger islands. The smaller islands appear uninhabited. Shorelines are irregular and indented but rarely big enough to form an anchorage. Much of this water is only three feet deep but with careful study of the chart and some courage one can leave the main channel and gunk-hole successfully so long as the wind remains gentle.

On across Charlotte Harbor and Boca Grande—comparatively large, wide open bodies of water—we sail northward toward Englewood where the chart shows a little pond labeled Cape Haze. We named it Cape Haze Hole. The waterway had narrowed to no more than a hundred yards when we pulled off to enter it and to discover that it was maybe a hundred yards in diameter, and completely surrounded by a three foot high, concrete bulkhead. Close beyond this were about fifteen very plain, large, ranch houses, each facing the water. The pond itself was absolutely empty of any object except water. Nothing to do but anchor in the middle and go below to hide while the residents of those dreary houses were probably staring out at us.

SUNDAY, JAN. 15: The waterway is still narrow, winding among patches of mangroves on our right, backed by somewhat dense, stunted oaks and quite a few houses. The barrier beach on our left, however, is populated by interesting beach houses nestled among low dunes, shrubs and native bushes all with the look of exclusive communities.

Next is the city of Venice where we had been warned about its three bridges. Both the city and its airport are on an island forcing the waterway to make a big jog eastward which, in turn, results in each of the three major highways serving the city to enter over a bascule bridge. The bridge-tenders seem to resent this. They are supposed to open every fifteen minutes but each times his opening precisely so that while you may wait only five to fifteen minutes for the first one, you arrive just as the next is beginning to close. The third bridge claims heavy auto traffic as an excuse to flout the fifteen minute rule also by closing as you arrive. It holds you and a fast-growing group of companions for as much as a half hour before commencing the nearly five-minute opening process. In total the delays amount to more than an hour.

Narrow Venice Inlet, a mile beyond these bridges, is quite attractive with large casuarina clumps and lush, irregular shorelines. It also feeds three elongated bays leading eastward into the mainland. Luckily the tidal rise here is not much more than a foot, otherwise this place would be a maelstrom of current pouring in and out daily from these large expanses of water.

Soon thereafter we have Siesta Key to port which is truly and quietly exclusive, and then we enter Sarasota's complex of harbors, bridges, islands—called keys—and 14-story high-rises all looking very civilized and somehow inviting. Marina Jack's, our destination, is right in the middle of all this. We cruise around a bit discovering where there might be room to anchor, where the gas dock and the marina office are, where there might be a dinghy-float, etc. The marina's extensive slips and shore facilities seem to divide the harbor into two big bays, one with perhaps thirty boats at anchor and the other empty except for one large sailboat near the bay's center, and a big Mississippi sternwheel dinner-boat at its pier. Why so empty? We circle around the sailboat trying to figure this out; why there might be some rule forbidding anchoring. But if so, why was this one boat here. The water depths throughout were ample. Ginger asks, "Does the dinner-boat need lots of room to back out of its slip?"

"Well, yes. That thing probably turns about as sharply as a locomotive, but there's still plenty of space!" So, down went the anchors and out came the little outboard for the dinghy. Just at dusk the dinner-boat's big paddle-wheel began to turn and, with a great deal of splashing it slowly backed out in a huge arc, not passing anywhere near us. What a perfect spot with the city rising behind us and islands to be explored spread out ahead.

The next morning we climbed into the dinghy and motored in, quickly found the dinghy float, tied up and went walking. Marina Jack's must have some big concession from the city as there is no competition anywhere in its vicinity. And competition would have a tough time; Jack's has it all. A large, free, parking lot, a sumptuous restaurant with a fancy bar and a second-story view, a well-stocked marine store, a small branch bank, small-boat day-rentals, the dinner-boat, and an outdoor (under cover) laundromat only a few yards from the marina slips.

Of course the latter had to be explored, looking for interesting sailing craft or looking at big, expensive ones; possibly also, running into other cruising owners like ourselves. Struck up a conversation with Louise Davis, returning to her Cheoy Lee Offshore 33 with the week's laundry. She and her husband have settled in for the winter with a car ashore, and a phone on board. He was at work, part time, for an engineering firm. It's likely that they'll stay all winter but, as she said, they could "shove off at any time." In no way are they shore-bound. They sail most weekends with one or two other couples they've met here at the marina. This seemed to us like the way we should do it next year; fetch up here for a month or so with a car and a phone. What more could one ask?

Ginger's sister Alice and husband, Art Backer, aren't due for another two days, during which there are a number of chores to do. First, off to the market to shop for four on board. After crossing the broad esplanade which borders the harbor, we walked a mile to a Wynn-Dixie (supermarket) which was OK going, but we hailed a cab for the return with four bags full. Next year: folding bikes.

When we were in Stuart I'd bought an electronic auto-pilot to ease our long hours at the helm. Often, also, if I'm steering in a narrow channel and the jib or something else up forward needs attention, I cannot leave the tiller for more than about twenty seconds and must call Ginger to come up from below to deal with it. Immediately the utility of this equipment was apparent but for the last ten days I have not been able to adjust it to our boat's movements and the machine was just not going to learn. I've wrapped it up to mail back to Stuart and, at the same visit to the post office, I hope to pick up our repaired depth sounder. In addition to the VHF radio, these are the only electronics on board and neither has worked satisfactorily. The depth sounder, installed new in Vineyard Haven has never read accurately in shallow water, just where we need it. I've made many long distance calls to the manufacturer's engineer and finally, several weeks ago, I sent it back to him.

After the cab delivered us and our groceries to the marina, I walked back to the post office and there was the depth sounder. Back at the boat I re-installed it, changed the engine's oil, refilled our kerosene lamps, and moved my stuff from the forward cabin to the port berth in the main cabin. Some other gear had to be moved and the two forward berths made up for our guests.

THURSDAY, JAN. 19: Alice and Art arrived right on schedule just before lunch so we took them directly to the marina's second floor restaurant where, by prior arrangement, we met Art's brother for a congenial lunch in this very nice place. Then A&A came aboard to get unpacked and settle in for the rest of the afternoon. Had to dinghy out in relays from the aluminum float beside the dinner-boat because the dinghy wouldn't hold four, plus luggage. Alice first worried about stepping into the dinghy and second, worried it would tip over.

The Backers are not boating people so the next morning was spent familiarizing them with the workings of their new abode. About four in the afternoon we departed for a short power trip south a few bridges where we found a small hole on the west shore in which to anchor. High mangroves and the dike of a bridge-approach provided shelter; an attractive spot. This is Little Sarasota Bay at White Beach on the south-eastern tail of Siesta Key.

The trip back to Pine Island Sound the next day was uneventful giving the Backers an opportunity to begin to relax, a light wind allowed us to sail on a broad reach most of the way. We decided to stop in at Cabbage Key for dinner and the night.

This small island is the site of author Mary Roberts Rinehart's house and big wooden water tower built in 1930 on an ancient Indian shell mound as her winter quarters. It's now an inn and restaurant.

The chart indicated that the approach to the island is all shallow requiring us to pass by at some distance and then make a sharp U-turn to follow a narrow, curving, dredged channel next to the shore. We took the sails down outside but the wind had piped up considerably after sunset so it was heads-up sailing even under power as we made the turn, guided only by an occasional small stake-marker. In a few minutes the old boat house hove into view, and there the channel abruptly ended. About six sailboats were already tied up nearly filling all the deep water space and we were approaching them fast.

Now, you can't just stop a boat and sit there while you figure something out. A decision had to be made quickly before we lost speed and steerage, and before the wind pushed us into the other boats. Luckily the manager was standing on the dock waving at us and pointing to the only space left. We slid in between two other boats with only a foot to spare on each side. I threw it into reverse, gave a blast of full throttle and *Lyla* stopped just as the bow touched the dock ahead. Touched? Well, banged lightly, and no one noticed. Ginger tossed him a bow line and I had managed to get a line around the up-wind piling alongside aft as we slid past it. Alice & Art just stayed out of the way.

A short walk up a winding path brought us to the big, white-washed, rustic-boarded house. It was nearly dark outside, but inside, all was mellow, knotty pine lit with dim, wrought-iron chandeliers overhead; just as it would have looked with kerosene lamps fifty years ago. The dining room was half full but voices were subdued by the peaceful atmosphere. We dallied over a most enjoyable dinner, the kind after which you hardly look at the check. The wind had died, foretelling a quiet night by the time the four of us walked back to the boat.

It seemed to us amazing that a restaurant and inn could survive all by itself out here in the middle of big Pine Island Sound with the neighboring islands appearing to have so few houses on them. Even Useppa has only about twenty. The only access to any of these islands is by private boat. No ferries or other public transport for miles. One feels very much alone sailing here compared to Florida's east coast. And the ratio of sail boats to sport-fishing-type power boats is reversed. However, this impression of isolation is misleading because these islands and the nearby mainland coast are all heavily wooded with mangrove, casuarina and scrub-pine so houses don't show much. We had no idea that 15-mile-long Pine Island a few miles to the north has a population of 9,000 while to the south are the major islands of Cayo Costa, N. Captiva, and Sanibel with more thousands of people, all within a half-hour powerboat ride to Cabbage Key.

SATURDAY, JAN. 21: Leaving Cabbage Key was easy compared to our entry the evening before. We sailed south with engine and mainsail only, as the Backers were still a bit nervous when the boat heeled to the wind. For their amusement and our curiosity, we decided to stop and explore one of the area's up-scale resorts, South Seas Plantation.

At the southern tip of Captiva we turned west into a hidden, little channel among high mangroves. Two more turns brought us to a fuel dock where a snappily-dressed attendant explained the facilities and entertainment available while we took on all the gas our tank would hold, just 6.8 gallons. I felt sure we appeared to be "the last of the big spenders." We then proceeded into a large and immaculate marina. Available were two 18-hole golf courses, hotel rooms, water-view cottages, lush condominiums, a top-rated dining room, ball room, three swimming pools, two squash courts, half a dozen tennis courts, deep-sea sport fishing boats for hire and, of course, an impressive gift shop. ("shop," hell! It was a complete department store.) I bought a new baseball cap which I wore for years until it finally fell apart. A&A disappeared for a while only to return to the boat for their tennis rackets; they'd talked themselves onto a court with two guests with whom they played for well over an hour.

After lunch we agreed that this had all been very nice but spending the night here would be prohibitively expensive. We'd cross San Carlos Bay and head back to the shelter of Shell Point Cove which we'd left only eight days before. Made it in over its threshold at about half tide just as darkness was closing in on us. The wind had come up out of the north so I set the anchors in hard and we slept well as the little cove remained calm though the wind was shaking the mast and I could feel the boat shifting around.

By morning the wind had dwindled and we watched the one other boat in the cove retrieve anchors and leave only to fetch up near the entrance. He backed off and tried several more times, each time stirring up great quantities of mud but getting nowhere. Evidently, the wind had blown most of the water out of the cove and into San Carlos Bay, but since we probably drew a foot or two less than he with our big centerboard retracted, we should be able to get out. Over we went to the threshold and thurrumff, into the mud. Backed off—with a struggle to get loose—and tried all along the threshold, several times getting stuck *hard* as the mud just would not let go. We must have spent an hour at it before giving up. Looking around the cove's shore I could see bare mud banks at least two feet high which obviously were usually under water. We compared notes with Julian, skipper of *Shearwater*, the other boat, deciding to just relax and wait. Flood tide was scheduled to begin about eleven o'clock. The tide-table forecast yesterday's tide as the lowest of the month but with last night's northeast wind having died, the water should already be rising fast.

We didn't get out until 2:15 PM. Made it under the Sanibel Bridge by four and into Fort Myers Beach at 5:15. After a comfortable night we departed a little after 9 AM, heading south, out in the Gulf, toward Marco Island. This was very ordinary sailing a mile or so off shore, close-hauled into a twelve-knot breeze. Occasional marker pilings, denoting the off-shore boundary of the Everglades National Park kept us on course while gentle rollers made *Lyla* pitch just enough to make Art seasick. Nothing to be done about this except get him to our destination as soon as possible.

By 1530 we were heading in and the water had turned from gray-green to the beautiful turquoise of the tropics. We'd just picked up (spotted) the Marco Island entrance buoy when the engine stopped with a jerk. I knew we'd caught something in the prop. If this had to happen, this was the perfect place. Crystal clear water, almost no wind on a warm afternoon.

I tried reversing the prop but no joy. Nothing to do but put on my shorts and dive overboard with my sheath-knife in my teeth. The culprit was a two-foot-diameter ball of shredded polypropylene line. I'd never seen such a thing. We sailors hate "poly" line for many reasons, and this was yet another; rope all torn apart and the fibers tangled into a great big rat's nest. I jammed the fingers of both hands into it, placed my feet against the keel and pulled. Nothing gave way. I had to spend at least fifteen minutes taking a deep breath, swimming down, hacking away with the knife, up for a breath and down again before it came free. We took it on board for disposal in the nearest trash can.

Pulled into a transient slip at the main marina, filled our water tanks and then went for a walk exploring. Art feeling just fine. The other boats were nearly all huge, high, sport-fishermen, fifty or sixty feet long. Everyone ashore seemed dressed by Ralph Lauren and very aloof. Everywhere there were high-rise condos and many buildings of ten stories or more. We cased the menus in the windows of several restaurants all with sky-high prices, shocking because food is cheap in Florida. In an hour we'd decided that Marco Island was all about MONEY.

Back at the boat we consulted. How about cruising up the river to that small town, Goodland, instead of staying here tonight? The chart was a bit mysterious in the vicinity of the high Marco bridge, showing many branching channels, some several miles long, and all likely infested with severe currents. But some "local knowledge" from the dock attendant resolved the uncertainty: "Just go under the big bridge, and then…don't look for that first can-buoy on the chart 'cause it's not there. Turn right 45° and head directly at the little island. And don't look for *it* on the chart because it's not *on* the chart. When you get real close, pass it on your left. You'll then see the next can-buoy way up ahead and you're on your way. It's easy; just follow the buoys to Goodland—and have fun!"

These instructions were faultless. An hour and a half later we came to a village with about 30 boats anchored in its open bay. This must be Goodland so we anchored among the boats in five and a half feet just as full darkness closed in. The moment the engine was shut off we realized what the dock attendant meant. Loud music with a pounding beat coming from a building ashore—though we were several hundred yards away—and car lights flashing on and off as traffic arrives or leaves. Loud voices carry over the water. A woman screams, then laughs. Somebody whistles. A motorcycle roars off into the night. It all sounded "real rough." We all went below for some good scotch in soft lamp-light and a home-cooked dinner with fresh bread Ginger had baked this morning.

TUESDAY, JAN. 23: The river had led us inland at least a mile so now we threaded our way through a maze of tiny islands in what the chart called "Coon Key Pass"; a series of narrow, twisting channels with depths of five to fifteen feet interwoven among these uninhabited keys. Just as we would begin to wonder which channel to take there would be a painted stake or a single, small buoy to guide us. In an hour we popped out into the Gulf. Partly cloudy with a wind just like yesterday but for the first time hot and humid. We've had to come all the way from New England to the Everglades to get warm. I set a course about a mile off the coast where we don't have to worry about going aground, but like yesterday we seem always to be drifting out farther and having to correct. A course change of 5° slowly angles us back in, and easing back to only a 2° change corrects for the drift. I finally wake up to realize that it's just a falling tide that's pushing us out.

The coast, though indented by many creeks and river mouths, actually shows no such details. Only continuous, high, impenetrable mangrove forest devoid of any sort of a landmark mile after mile. Even with the aid of the charts and binoculars nothing smaller than the biggest rivers can be discerned. I call out "We should be passing Everglade City which has a river opening big enough for large freighters. Can anyone see anything along shore?"

Silence.

Finally Alice says, "I think I see a big, dead tree-trunk, and the trees next to it look slightly darker green than those a few hundred yards or so south."

"OK, that must be it. The city is two miles inland but I'd expected to see *something more obvious!*"

About 5 PM some sort of distinct irregularity in the shoreline finally appeared, and our time and speed figures indicate that we must be nearing the Little Shark River so we headed in. A hump on the straight, dark line of the horizon began to take shape as a large clump of very tall trees. Through the binocular we could make out many, huge, bleached, white trunks of dead trees. A park boundary piling showed up which must be one shown on the chart two miles out from Little Shark. Two miles out and the water is only fifteen feet deep?! The chart also showed a small floating day-mark way in next to the river mouth to which we set a course and soon discovered that the bow was pointed right at the end of the tall trees. The buoy didn't appear until we were within a half mile of it because it turned out to be a dirty brown with no contrast to the greenish-gray water. Now the river mouth was discernible. Its outflow had evidently scoured out a channel as the water deepened to twenty feet. This is a substantial river with ten foot-high banks topped by dense jungle. A hundred yards inside we passed three cruising sailboats at anchor but we carried on exploring. I was hoping to reach the entrance to Whitewater Bay some ten miles long. Arriving at an intersection after about a mile, I chose to go right but in fifty yards the jungle trees and mangrove squeezed so close to us that our rigging was about to snag on the branches. There was just no way through for a boat bigger than a canoe. I had to back out before there was even room to turn around. The other branch at the intersection was wider but still walled in by mangrove and dense trees way above our masthead. There was less current running here so we put down two anchors which I buoyed as I suspected that the bottom was laden with fallen trunks and branches. (A small buoy with a line attached to the head of an anchor enables one to recover it upside down.)

The moment the boat stopped we were pounced on by clouds of mosquitoes and no-see-ums. I was frantic before I got the anchors set. We all rushed below, closed everything and sprayed with a bug-bomb. The portholes all have screens but we had to set up the special, large ones I'd made for the companionway and the forward hatch. The tiny no-see-ums were squeezing through so we coated every screen with Avon Skin So Soft, the best insect repellent known to man. (Sadly, this bath oil's scent is cheap and cloying; as someone said, "it makes you smell worse than a French whore." But it works!) The hot, humid air inside was unbearable but soon there were no live insects left in the cabin and we could open portlights and hatches.

The next morning we awoke to a great darkness in the cabin. No light was coming through our screens. Every one was completely coated with layers of dead mosquitoes stuck to the gooey Skin So Soft! And now, we were going to have to slather that stuff on our arms and faces before we dared go outside.

None too soon we were out of the Little Shark and on our way south to Cape Sable, the southernmost point of mainland Florida, where we took a point-of-departure south for 27 nautical miles in the ocean. A course of 172° included a correction for westerly current. We are holding a precise heading in order to pass John Sawyer Key closely to avoid a three-foot spot shortly thereafter. Actually the Seven Mile Bridge appeared long before we raised the little key but it allowed us to correct our position exactly. Though the bridge is huge, there is only one section high enough for us to pass under it before turning east to Marathon.

Shortly after 3 PM we made the turn and headed into the narrow entrance of Boot Key Harbor. This is quite a place, a narrow, nearly two-mile-long slot with a very large marina, all sorts of marine services and several hundred boats. It's part of the village of Marathon, on Vaca Key, two thirds of the way down the Florida Keys. Boot Key

Marina is just the sort of facility which we like to avoid not only because there's too much noise and confusion—*but*, should there be a storm, too much risk of damage from other boats tied up too closely by perhaps unskilled owners.

Way up the harbor near its eastern end, we discovered Sombrero Resort where we tied up at first to their bulkhead along with about six other sail boats; but after one day we tired of the exhaust fumes from cars parked nose-in, no more than fifteen feet from us. By the next afternoon we'd learned the ropes, including the fact that we were welcome to anchor off and still make use of the resort's facilities.

Across the narrow harbor, next to the shelter of a big grove of high mangroves, were five boats anchored out. Ideal from our point of view since it would take no more than three minutes to dinghy in to the resort's waterside bar, laundromat, fuel, and local boaters' gathering spot. This is not a marina; it just has plans to become one. Just to the east the harbor narrows to a canal which, in about a mile, ends at a shopping center. Ginger can hop in the dinghy, start the outboard and in fifteen minutes tie up a few yards from the Publix Supermarket's side door.

THURSDAY, FEB. 8: We've been here for two weeks, the four of us taking day-trips by boat to explore other keys, or renting a car to explore the more distant Key West and keys surrounded by very shallow water. One day we went through Sister's Creek, the shortest way to the Atlantic, and on out to Sombrero Reef for skin-diving. Beautiful, clear water but the reef was a disappointment; all the coral is dead. Perhaps I'm spoiled after diving in the South Pacific during WW II. The swimming was great, however, and I took the opportunity to inspect the boat's bottom for fouling and the anti-electrolysis zinc.

Another day we went looking for a nice beach. Here we are in the Keys; there should be a nice beach. Several possible places were private, but then we followed a road shown on our chart as leading to a beach when suddenly we were in a town dump. Trash and battered appliances lay half buried in the sand. Fearing for the car's tires we continued, rounding a clump of casuarinas and there was the greatest little beach without a soul on it. We all piled out of the car stepping carefully over some cans and bottles to discover…broken glass! The entire beach was strewn with broken beer bottles shattered into little pieces, half buried in beautiful, white sand; razor-sharp edges sparkling in the sunlight!

A&A found the resort's tennis courts right away. I'd ferry them in to the dock and they'd walk to the courts where, either they'd stand around quietly with their racquets or they'd walk onto an empty court and begin to play. Since they are very good players, they are soon noticed and invited to make up a foursome with resort guests.

Two days ago their return-air reservations put an end to their visit. They managed to squeeze into the dinghy with me and their luggage while we motored to the shopping center, and there I loaded them into a cab for the airport, only another mile away. Easy! But we were sad to see them go. Ginger and her sister are very close and the four of us enjoy being together. California is so far away.

For weeks now our Nautisport inflatable dinghy has been springing air-leaks and I've been unable to keep up with patching them—the adhesive wasn't working very well. Too often, in the morning I'd look astern and discover the poor thing lying all deflated in the water and I'd then be faced with early exercise on the foot-pump. It *is* eight years old. I've ordered a replacement from Boat-US in New York; who knows how long it will take U.P.S. to deliver it. The bar manager and each of his waitresses have been told to *please accept it!* when it comes, so I hope nothing goes wrong. In another two days I'll start checking with them every day. This is one of the little problems with being a live-aboard; we have no address of our own!

FRIDAY, FEB. 10: To occupy some of the waiting time, we've decided to sail up to Flamingo, the National Park's big Everglades facility, a "voyage" of about forty miles. Everyone at the bar certainly knows we're waiting for the new dinghy, so just now, I've told Vicky, the lead waitress that we will be away for two days.

The first part of the trip is a reverse of our arrival in this area—westward down Boot Key Harbor, back under the Seven-mile Bridge and then sailing north for three hours to the southern tip of mainland Florida. Here we made a turn east around First National Bank and headed for Flamingo.

So far we have been at the western and now the northern edge of Florida Bay, a huge but very thin body of water dotted with dozens of small, uninhabited keys and sand bars each one with a name, often amusing: Black Betsey Key, Minor Key, Major Key. Elbow Bank, Sandy Bank and First National Bank. Big Bight, Mosquito Bight and Snake Bight. Some are so slightly above high tide that they can support only scraggly salt-grass. Others, a foot or so higher, are covered with low mangrove. The bay is twenty miles wide by almost forty miles long and most of it is no more than four feet deep. Rarely is it as deep as eight. We're passing and slowly closing with the south coast of Florida which appears as a thin, dark line on our left, a mile or so away. A high standpipe, seven miles along this line, stands out brightly in the late afternoon sun designating our destination. According to the chart there is also a much taller microwave tower but it must be too skinny to see.

The Flamingo entrance finally appeared only as some sort of human construction until we got very close and a small cut in the shoreline emerged. Inside this opening and to our left was a marina of just a dozen slips, nicely sheltered by trees and the ever-present mangroves. We slid into an empty slip. The pier itself was concrete but the finger-floats were aluminum; not too substantial nor long enough for a boat much larger than *Lyla*. For a big national park it all seemed too small. Surprising also was that, of the five other boats, only one was a power-boat and *Lyla* was the biggest vessel present. No human being was visible in the little office at the pier-head so we set off on foot in the direction of a large building a hundred yards inland.

Confronting us was a huge park of many acres, a great sweep of open land now covered with wild, coarse grass, low bushes and some nondescript, modern structures. We crossed an expanse of car-parking and, as we approached the biggest building, we realized that many long parking spaces had been set aside for busses; only about a dozen cars and one lone bus were currently present. It all had rather a deserted feeling.

The big building *did* turn out to be Park Headquarters. Inside, we found ourselves in a typical visitors' center; a long information counter with little stacks of literature on it, and a wall-sized map behind it but no Park Ranger. An adjoining section boasted several dioramas of Everglades flora and fauna. Further along we came upon a very large dining room with a bar and a stage set up for an orchestra. "Just like downtown" but in the middle of the Everglades?! There were half a dozen people at the bar and more having dinner. The occasional little clatter of dishes seemed louder than the sum of their voices. Retreating outside again we found another path leading to and around a pond about an acre in size, good for an evening walk and perhaps we'd see some wild life. Yes, a great blue (heron) at the far end, a few cattle egrets, some gulls in the water looking over their shoulders at us as they paddled away, and last, an ordinary pair of mallards. Not another human being to be seen anywhere on this vast expanse. In the distance there were other buildings, two-stories with many windows; perhaps condos? Time to go back to the boat; Ginger had chicken soup muttering gently on the stove.

In the middle of the night someone's foot or something landed on the deck right overhead! We both woke with a start. A scratching sound moving toward the cockpit. Quietly, I arose and grabbed our big flashlight. It was a big and fat raccoon. He'd smelled the soup, of course. He stared at the light for a long minute, his eyes bright red, before giving up and jumping off. The soup was put in the ice-box though still a bit warm.

SATURDAY, FEB. 11: Yesterday we'd learned that there is a tour boat—*The Bald Eagle*—to take one into the Everglades so this morning we found it just around the corner from our marina and we've climbed aboard. It's an open, very beamy launch with a sun roof and big enough to accommodate a whole bus-load of people but today we've joined only about a dozen. Its flat bottom enables it to draw only about a foot and it's propelled by a jet-nozzle which does not get entangled with submerged roots. The tour began right on time and in a few minutes we were in the deep shade of both black and red mangrove trees which closed completely overhead. Just a little, dappled sunlight broke through. We'd been warned to slather up with repellent but the mosquitoes were really not bad. I'd bet that the park sprays regularly.

We learned that mangrove thrives in a mix of fresh and salt water; the red excludes salt, the black and the white excrete salt. The guide was pointing out various flora and one fauna, a four-inch spider in its web. There *were* a number of wild flowers but most had to be pointed to before we noticed them. She kept saying that we'd surely see a big, freshwater alligator and just perhaps a cotton-mouth or two. Finally, she got her wish: about seven feet long and nearly submerged in a mud pool. It didn't move even an eyelid as we passed close by.

By evening we felt that we'd "done" Flamingo. It was a little disappointing and disconnected. It seemed that the chief attractions were deep-sea big-game fishing, camping out, or serious week-long canoe trips into the far reaches of the Everglades, none of which met our interests. We'd hoped to learn more about the Everglades than was available at the visitors' center diorama or "The Bald Eagle," and we'd expected to see numerous birds and several new species for our list, but no.

Sunday we retraced our course back to our Sombrero anchorage; a nice, easy sail and an opportunity to experiment with the auto-pilot. This foot-long box of electronics is secured on a cockpit seat with a small bracket. Protruding from one end is a substantial, steel rod which connects to the tiller and pushes or pulls it to guide the boat right or left according to instructions from its own compass. There is a large knob on top with which one sets a course; it's very sensitive and can be tweaked to adjust for just one degree. But, since there is much more to guiding a sailboat through the waves than just setting a course, and since each sailboat has a unique reaction to a wave or the wind, or both, the autopilot's electronics consist of complex programming and three internal adjusting screws that affect its reaction-time, the speed of the rod's thrust and what is labeled as Overshoot/Undershoot. I'm beginning to get the hang of it but it will be a month or so before the machine learns about our boat—not a lot longer than it takes a person to get the feel of a particular boat.

As soon as the anchors were down I dinghied over to the Sombrero Bar to ask if our new dinghy had arrived. No one seemed to know anything about it! It wasn't until the next day, Monday, that I learned that it had arrived by U.P.S. but a new waitress had refused to accept it! Oh no! I couldn't believe it. I had to call Boat-US in New York and re-order it. Now, we'd have to wait another week or so! Finally it came Thursday afternoon, ten days later.

During this enforced wait we found plenty to do. We had learned that good friends from The Vineyard were on their boat *Papillon* at Boot Key Marina. We made contact by VHF radio and they dinghied up to us for dinner one night. Then the Thomases radioed us that they were coming into Boot Key and they came over for drinks. We joined them on an overnight excursion to Newfound Harbor at Bahia Honda Key where we anchored off a beautiful half-moon beach. Met Merrill and Beth Hoyle on *Merribeth*. We all went swimming in the clear, turquoise water, and after dinner watched a huge bonfire that others had built from driftwood on the beach.

Another day we went snorkeling on the reef out in the Atlantic near Looie Key where I scrubbed moss off the boat's bottom. Then there's always boat maintenance: wear and tear repairs, painting and varnishing, changing the engine's oil, checking and cleaning its distributor and spark-plugs, and the outboard's plug.

FRIDAY, FEB. 24: The new, inflatable dinghy is a big improvement! We tore open the box, unrolled it, inflated it, installed the floorboards while it lay right on the dock next to the bar, various observers crowding around to watch. Someone helped me carry the old one to the bar's dumpster and I rowed the new one out to *Lyla*. The early inflatables were difficult to row. This one is a delight.

This morning we are off on our way north, up the chain of keys toward Miami. Halfway down Boot Key Harbor we turned into Sisters' Creek. Impenetrable, high mangroves on our right side and pretty houses with nice landscaping along the shore on our left—the most attractive part of Marathon—and fifteen minutes later we were running north in the Atlantic. We want to explore the inside passage on the Florida Bay side of the Keys so we are heading for "Channel Five," one of only three places in the 150 mile length of the Keys where a boat with a mast higher than nineteen feet can pass through the Florida Keys highway.

FRIDAY, 1600 hrs: Had a rather gentle sail, close-hauled to Channel Five, through the big bascule bridge and now we're anchored off the southwest shore of Lignumvitae Key where it's just six feet deep over a hard-coral bottom. At first the anchors wouldn't bite at all so I swam down to each one and managed to get their points dug in a little. So long as the wind doesn't come up much we'll be OK.

Lignumvitae Key is botanically interesting. We've just spent two hours hiking all over the little island with a state botanist telling us about every plant, tree and soil condition. Its three-quarter-mile length sports a dense forest of sub-tropical hardwoods including lignumvitae trees one of which is about 1,600 years old. An extremely dense and oily wood weighing 80 pounds per cubic foot, it is still used for certain heavy-machinery bearings. Because the wood has been quite rare and dear for 200 years, this forest has been protected since about 1800. Besides a small State Park building and a pier there are no other structures on the island and visits are restricted to three days a week.

SATURDAY, FEB 25: Onward north in east Florida Bay past the Matecumbe Keys and into an area where skinny, sort of crumpled chains of tiny islets appear to attach twenty-four-mile-long Key Largo to the mainland by surrounding first Buttonwood Sound, then Blackwater, Barnes and Card Sounds and finally Biscayne Bay.

These key-chains remind me of nothing so much as lumpy necklaces tossed down on someone's bureau-top. While they are fragile-looking on a chart, they are covered with dense, high mangroves which appear to wall off each of the above bodies of water which are two to four miles across. Narrow channels cut through each chain and allow passage from one sound to the next. At each there is yet another deep-sea-fishing marina surrounded by honky-tonk strip development—not appealing to us.

We made it into and through Barnes Sound just as the sun was setting. A hard coral bottom again made anchoring tricky near Turkey Point just east of the channel, and the traffic noise was horrendous. So we turned around, sailed west about a mile and found quiet shelter behind the mangroves from a rising north wind, and a softer bottom as well. Strange that no one else took advantage of this. Not another boat in sight; they're all in the marina!

This morning we are heading up toward Biscayne Bay fighting at least two knots of foul current. Started without sail but were indicating only about four knots against the north wind. Subtract the current and our actual headway was no more than two knots, so I set the main, strapped it in tight and felt better when our headway increased to about four. Our course was too close into the wind to carry the jib.

Shortly after entering Biscayne Bay we dropped the main and headed for a private canal called the Pines, at the end of which a good friend from the Vineyard has a condo. He wasn't in residence now and near the entrance we could see what looked like big estates and a big PRIVATE! sign so we kind of chickened out, turned around and motored south into No Name Harbor at Key Biscayne's southern tip. It was chockablock full of boats, all on anchors and too close together; sure-trouble in the night, so back we went to The Pines.

Once we were inside, it looked less private; a quarter-mile-long, narrow canal bordered on the north by pretty houses and on the south by the high, dense mangroves and pines of a state forest. In the distance ahead to the east, was our friend's 12-story high-rise. Several sailboats were anchored bow-out from the forest with a line to a mangrove astern. We followed suit. All was serene and quiet; a beautiful spot! The canal ended at a tiny beach less than a hundred yards away. Our friend had informed us, "Hide your dinghy under the sea-grape bush there, walk up the steps and you'll be right down town. All the shops you'll need plus a good movie house." Anchored on our starboard side was *Jalan-2*, a Westsail 32 with a nice young couple and two little girls aboard, from Newtown, Connecticut! Spent two days here exploring Key Biscayne on foot, and by a bus which runs up and down the length of Biscayne Boulevard. Shopped at Publix, found kerosene for our lamps, replenished our cash at a bank and enjoyed some sightseeing.

On Wednesday we headed north to Miamarina intent on renting a car to explore Miami. Miamarina is very large and though it is next to the city's center it is nicer than we expected. Having arrived a little after lunch we spent the afternoon exploring it and the adjacent Bayside Park. Needing Scotch for our evening cocktail we crossed the street west of the park looking for a liquor store and, to our surprise, found no one who spoke English. Here in the center of a major American city we were having trouble making ourselves understood! Cubans have taken over.

Retreating back to the marina we went looking for cruising boats—as differentiated from floating, weekend cabins—and perhaps interesting people aboard them. The slips are of ample size and sailboats are grouped together. All the services that one needs are available including a laundromat with twelve machines, car rentals and a first class restaurant upstairs with a panoramic view.

We met Peggy and Wentworth Fling aboard *Highland Fling*, their 38-foot *Invicta*. A nice couple, older than we who live on Long Island, N.Y. He is "determined to stay young by sailing as much of every year as possible." The boat is old and dark below, from a previous generation of ocean-going vessels. It is crammed with the gear and the wear of many years—Peggy tagging along with a stoic upper lip. She misses all her friends at home and craved social contact. They are trying to talk us into going to the Bahamas; they are all set to leave.

We had previously decided not to attempt this *this* year feeling that we needed more seasoned experience but they kept saying "Just follow along with us. This will be our eleventh trip." Later they came aboard for drinks and we realized that their experience would be invaluable and that we should take them up on it. The next morning we rented a car again and went off shopping for food and supplies for at least a week. We did have on board a *Bahamas Chart-kit* with all the necessary charts, and we were up till ten o'clock pouring over Kline's *The Yachtsman's Guide to the Bahamas*.

In the morning, since we still had the car, we drove down to Cocoanut Grove and visited Villa Vizcaya, a somewhat smaller but more sophisticated version of Hearst's Castle in California. This was an adventure which we recommend to anyone sight-seeing in Miami. The huge mansion of three floors is furnished with antiques, oriental rugs and tapestries in the best of taste, and is surrounded by three formal gardens each of an individual style. Its waterfront was originally a swamp with a limestone rock in the middle almost 100 feet long and at least ten feet high. With an intent to receive guests arriving from their yachts, the swamp was dredged and artisans brought in to carve the limestone lump into a huge barge with ornate, Italianate stairs and railings enclosing three decks at different heights for entertaining or just viewing Biscayne Bay. The island remained "offshore" so we could imagine liveried oarsmen waiting to transport guests across the 30 feet of water to the gardens, and the big main house.

Back at the boat we were relaxing with an evening drink when the radio came alive with, "*Lyla, Lyla*...this is *Highland*, over." I picked up the mike and answered. It was Peggy explaining that some emergency at Wentworth's business had occurred requiring him to fly to New York thus delaying their Bahamas trip. Peggy was to remain on board. Furthermore, we should depart on our own and they would catch up in a day or two.

Well, this was just what we didn't want to hear, but after some discussion we decided to go. We'd sail right back to The Pines Canal in the morning, spend the night there and get an early start south to Fowey Rocks where we could lay a better course across the 44 nautical miles of Gulf Stream to tiny Gun Cay. The only significant factor in question would be the amount of course-correction to offset the Gulf Stream current. Several people had each said that plotting the current drift at 2½ knots would bring us close enough to the low cay that we would surely see it so we began to feel more confident. Of course the correctness of a 2½ knot average depends on the wind and how long it takes us to cross; the longer we are in the current the more we will be set to the north. Also, should the wind die, say, for an hour or so while we were near the axis of the stream where the current is strongest we'd have to add more correction.

WEDNESDAY, MARCH 7: Shortly after 7 AM we were on our way to Fowey Rocks. South of Key Biscayne is a large expanse of open but shallow water; so shallow, in fact, that a number of houses have been built on stilts as much as several miles from any shore. We took a point of departure from Cape Florida on the southern tip of Key Biscayne through this area to a flashing, four-second red two miles southeast and clear of the shoals, then five more miles south to the big buoy at Fowey Rocks. There was plenty of wind out there, almost too much for the genny but then it was on the beam and likely to remain from the south-west so we did not shorten sail, settling on to a course of 119°. Directly astern, in the distance, were the tall buildings south of Miami so I selected two of the highest which were in line on our 119° course to use as a current indicator. For the next two hours, which would bring us to the axis of greatest current, I could see exactly what the current was doing to us by adjusting course to keep the buildings in line. At first a 25° correction was way too much. But slowly I watched the current increase and as the buildings finally disappeared over the horizon I was using 18° to keep them in line. About six hours later, in twenty-five knots of wind and four-foot seas, the little lighthouse of Gun Cay poked above the horizon looking like a tiny thorn just a bit to the south of our course—I should have reverted to a 20° correction.

There was too much wind and sea to head up to douse the genny so, with the main boom "wung" way out, I managed to pull it down in the shadow of the main and lash the flogging sail to the lifeline as we closed with Gun Cay and avoided the barely visible brown bar en route to Cat Cay. We'd averaged nearly seven knots for the crossing! Tied up at one of several Cat Cay piers and I went ashore to find the customs officer. No one except the skipper is allowed ashore until a vessel has "cleared in."

In the yellow building ahead of our pier I found the customs officer who marched me back to *Lyla* and directly went below to sit with his papers—as stiff and formal as his uniform. Though the procedure was minimal his demeanor was that of a consul conducting a treaty between two nations. Any pets on board were never to be allowed on shore, bicycles must be declared and registered and we *must* clear customs when we depart.

Cat Key, barely two miles long, a few hundred yards wide and quite heavily wooded is owned by the Rockwell Corporation which has created a little jewel of a resort for the use of its employees. A breakwater completes a surrounding enclosure for the piers which reach out from a pristine, narrow, white-sand beach. Several substantial buildings containing a gift shop, small market, Bahamas customs, port operations and administration hide in the shade of carefully clipped mangroves. Further around the curving beach I noticed a line of lush condos amidst many palm trees.

Thursday we loafed, exploring the island and hoping that the Flings would catch up to us. Ginger saw a large stingray with big, brown and yellow spots with white centers in the tiny surf of the beach. We were somewhat apprehensive about our next passage across "The Banks" to Chub Cay.

The Bahamas Islands rest on four, flat, submerged, coral plateaus or "banks" which are typically about fifteen feet below the surface but drop off abruptly at their edges to the ocean abyss hundreds of fathoms deep. Bimini, Gun Cay and Cat Cay are on the western edge of Great Bahama Bank. Yesterday, just offshore from Gun Cay we watched the ocean change from inky, dark blue and 462 fathoms deep to turquoise at less than a fathom in half a minute.

We are now about to undertake a 75-mile sail, out of sight of land for many hours, to the bank's eastern edge at Tongue-of-the-Ocean where the water shoals to a fathom and is infested with coral heads reaching almost to the surface. There will be no navigation aids along the course except Russell, which is only a small, rotting wooden platform, its light not functioning, a mile north of our course. Finally, when we arrive at the bank's eastern edge, we must find the Northwest Channel Beacon and pass it close aboard in order to avoid the coral heads. The water color will again change to inky blue as we pass over the edge and the depth will drop vertically to 605 fathoms—3630 feet! From there it's another fourteen miles across Tongue-of-the-Ocean to Chub Cay.

Accosting anyone inclined to talk to us as we wander about Cat Cay, two people tell us that it's best to start across about dusk in order to arrive at the beacon in full daylight. They described it as a rusty little tower about twenty feet high with a light, if working, which cannot be seen at night as far away as the tower itself in daylight. The tidal currents will be across our course at about half a knot at max, they told us.

Remember, this is 1983—no GPS, and Loran is still very expensive so one has only Radio Direction Finder (RDF) or celestial as navigation aids.

It's Friday afternoon and we've not heard from the Flings. At five PM we depart, line up with Gun Cay lighthouse astern in the sunset, course 098° magnetic. Low tide is at about 6:30 PM so the first three hours should result in no drift. There's a light wind stirring up a light chop so we have the engine on at 1300 rpm to help us along.

We'll take turns at the helm for about four hours each with the assistance of the auto pilot, while the other one of us sleeps. Looks like a comfortable if rather slow passage.

A three-quarter moon came up after several hours and twice we saw a dim light in the distance which seemed to get no closer as it passed abeam and then slowly faded away behind us. We hoped these were just Bahamian fishermen, not pirates. Nothing whatever else to be seen except clouds passing the face of the moon, phosphorescence from our bow wave and the dim red light on the compass dial. Depths still 6 to 14 feet. It wasn't strange that we should have pirates on our minds. Druggies had begun to take advantage of the Bahamas' remoteness for transfers and deliveries of their wares, and only a few months before there had been a story in the news about a sailing vessel being boarded, its crew murdered and the boat found deserted many weeks later.

At 2:25 AM Saturday we anchored for a few minutes to take a number of RDF bearings. Chub and Bimini made sense indicating our position as a mile south of our dead reckoning course. Freeport was a sloppy fix and Grand Bahama's signal was unusable. In another half hour we had run out our time to Russell so turned north to correct our doubtful RDF position. After twenty minutes something appeared in the beam of our spotlight. We headed over to inspect and found four rotten piles protruding out of the water, one with a piece of an anglebrace still hanging on it. The remainder of the Russell platform had disappeared.

With Russell as a new departure point we laid a new DR course and at 5:19 we spotted the Northwest Channel Light, passed it to starboard half an hour later, noted the change in the water color as we passed over the edge of the bank and changed course for Chub Cay. With the wind out of the northeast at about twelve knots we were close-hauled but the chop was light and the day was shaping up to be sunny; the sky dotted with puffy little white clouds.

In two hours we arrived at Chub, a skinny island about three miles long with a big pond in its midsection. At the eastern end is Chub Resort & Marina in a man-made basin. We entered through its zigzag channel to gas up, investigate its facilities and check whether the Flings were there. The place was built by the British shortly before the

Bahamas were turned over to the Bahamians. It now looked as if it had been deteriorating ever since, threadbare and faded. Everywhere the coarse grass, which had once been a lawn was growing into the paths and roads. All the features one might expect to find at a resort were present but closed. The lobby of the main building looked used and there was a Bahamian woman behind the hotel-type front desk, but not another human being in sight. A large dining room opened off one side where three tables were set but at least a dozen more were bare. Turned out that only dinner was served and only three days a week unless one reserved ahead. The bar was open nightly but if no one showed up by 8 PM it closed. The pool was reserved for guests but since we had a *yacht* in the marina—and there were few guests—we were invited to use it if we desired.

The Flings didn't appear for two more days so we decided to prevent the bar from closing before we'd had a few drinks each evening. No need to hurry in the morning either. Finally on Tuesday the 13th the Flings arrived too late and tired to carry on to Nassau. But Wednesday dawned cloudy and pleasant, and a nice breeze of about twelve knots came up with enough north in it to allow us to lay our course not quite close-hauled. Wentworth set the latter at about 118° with his Loran so we just kept him in sight all the way. The deep blue of the very deep Tongue-of-the-Ocean can only be described as inky.

Landfall—the western end of New Providence Island—appears more than two hours before one arrives at Nassau's harbor entrance so we were feeling impatient long before the big hotels made square bumps on the horizon. Next the lighthouse and then the huge breakwater appears ahead. The entrance is fairly narrow but quickly opens out at the harbor's NW end to about a half-mile wide where one passes all the cruise-ship and freighter berths to starboard, and long, thin, forested Paradise Island to port. Next, to starboard, is the city itself dominated by oddly shaped Fincastle Tower rising above the other high-rises. As Paradise continues to squeeze closer, the harbor narrows to less than a quarter mile at its SE end where the bridge crosses to Paradise and where several marinas are located. From the lighthouse to the last marina it's over two miles long.

Once we'd passed the big ship docks we saw that there was great anchoring space all along the Paradise shore. Good shelter is created by the tall buildings and hills on the city side and the high trees and higher hotels on the other. For nearly a mile many cruising boats, mostly sail, were anchored, many of considerable size and interest. We found a comfortable space among them, set our two anchors in glass-clear water and after surveying our surroundings inflated our dinghy to row around hoping to glean local knowledge from neighboring vessels. Roused several people happy to feed us info, such as: are there any special harbor rules we must follow? How safe is it to leave our boat while we explore ashore? Where is it safe to leave our dinghy while we walk into town? What and where are the interesting places to visit? Where is a market with the best prices for ice and the few foodstuffs we might need? Which is the best marina and how to find it? Is its gasoline pure? Is there a qualified engine mechanic? Where's the best water and is there a charge? The best marine hardware supply? Any tricks to departing the SE end of the harbor for the Exumas?

Some interesting answers: no strange harbor rules. Don't anchor near the Bahamasair seaplane ramp; the noise from arriving aircraft is horrendous. Not safe to leave one's boat. They sneak on board and carry off anything of value in ten minutes. We all watch each other's boats. Just drop by and notify one of us when and how long you will be ashore. Leave your dinghy at the Lighthouse Station dock where you will see other dinghies. This is the safest with rare exceptions. Or spend an hour at the Art Gallery, cozy up to the owner and ask whether you may *chain* your dinghy to his bulkhead where he can keep an eye on your outboard. The tourist area of the city and the shopping area near the marinas are otherwise safe. Prices are better near the latter. Don't try to buy fish or conch at Potter's Key—in fact stay away from it. Visit the Governor's mansion and take a bus NW out to the zoo. Dinghy into the canal in Paradise to experience the lush-life in the posh hotels and perhaps swim at one of the beautiful beaches if you're dressed like a rich tourist. Yacht Haven Marina is the favorite. Their gas is usually OK. Sometimes there's water in it and sometimes it's discarded avgas that's so loaded with lead that it will foul your plugs. Water is free and is quite good; top off your tanks at any slip but not at the gas dock where it's not so good. Be careful working your way out the east end along Rose Island; some of the courses in the *Bahamas Guide* are enough off to run you into a coral head—make up your own range using Fincastle as you return there from the Exumas. Et cetera! All this and more from the crews of just two boats, and we made some new friends. What a lot of troubles we avoided.

As we made our way into Yacht Haven the next day there was *Ayuthia* in a slip. After getting gas, and with our fenders in place, we slid in quietly to surprise the Grews as we rafted up along side. Great fun exchanging adventures since we'd seen them in Georgetown, South Carolina. We got out our water hose, stretched it across *Ayuthia* to the slip faucet and let our tanks fill as we talked. Later we discovered the Clarks anchored in the little bight between the seaplane ramp and the bridge. Their home is two houses from ours in Vineyard Haven. I neglected to write their boat's name in the Log, and now I can't recall it.

THURSDAY, MARCH 15: Dinghied into Nassau and managed to find the Art Gallery's little wharf because there were four dinghies tied up to it. This stretch of waterfront consists of many small businesses jammed together along the edge of about a six-foot bank, each with some sort of cobbled-together pier or bulkhead. Many outboard-powered launches and skiffs continually poke in and out. We tied up as recommended with quarter-inch chain, and, with some misgivings, made our way up to the gallery. Once inside we discovered that our friend David Aiken had several of his paintings here for sale. With this introduction we were accepted by the owner who agreed to keep an eye out his window where he could see our outboard, and we took off exploring.

Nassau is a city predominately of three or four story wood or concrete-block buildings. Just a few high rises are scattered among them. Its busy center has a dozen substantial government buildings and a fancy main street along which are at least thirty stores catering to well-to-do tourists and the small, local upper class. High-style, black Bahamian women, dressed right out of Vogue clack by on four-inch heels. At intersections, equally high-styled police in wide, white, Sam Browne belts wheel and wave instructions to oncoming traffic. Street vendors in brightly colored dresses hawk souvenirs to tourists from the huge cruise ships docked not a hundred yards away—all this in a sort of controlled pandemonium. Beyond this center, poverty closes in abruptly, forming a broad surrounding fringe of sun-bleached, worn, gray housing and small shops. However, with many trees offering welcome shade, tropical, green hills rising behind the big, gray, white or pink government houses, the magnificent harbor, and reggae's thumping beat echoing from somewhere, Nassau is quite attractive.

On Friday we found the right bus to take us out to the zoo and spent a comparatively quiet morning watching the animals. Back at the boat we dinghied into a canal through the jungle forest of Paradise to one of its ten-story hotels, all looking just like Disneyland or a movie set—an immaculate, make-believe Bahamas. Since we were wearing neither Gucci nor a paisley shirt we felt slightly out of place as we wandered through the ornate, high-ceilinged hotel lobby and adjoining expensive shops.

FRIDAY, MARCH 16: We've made some plans. We'll call our old sailing friends, the Wests in Vineyard Haven, to join us at a marina on Grand Bahama Island and from there sail with us back to West Palm Beach in Florida. There are half a dozen flights a day into Grand Bahama's airport and it's then only a short cab ride to that marina.

Telephoning in the Bahamas usually entails going to a call center which resembles a small bus station. There are rows of seats in a large room and an iron-barred window at one end where one obtains a ticket from the agent and pays a fee based on the call's destination. Then you take a seat, wait for your ticket number to be called and told which of the several doorless booths you are to use. The wait is on Bahamas time, i.e., there is no sense of hurry, no such thing as a waste of time. You may sit for five minutes or half an hour. There are often more empty booths than those in use. And there's almost no conversation among those waiting, no sign of impatience—just quietly sitting. Eventually you are told to go to a booth, pick up the receiver and wait again for your connection to go through.

Rather than endure this, I got in the dinghy, motored back to the Paradise Island hotel, walked into its lobby, quickly found a modern phone booth and direct-dialed to the Wests. So much for that! They accepted immediately.

We are to meet in nine days, during which we'll have time to sail 35 miles down to Highborne Cay to experience what the Exumas are like, turn around and return to Nassau before heading for Grand Bahama. On our way, we'll cruise through the Berry Islands to Great Harbor Cay. And from there we'll take a point of departure and navigate 66 nautical miles of open sea to the south coast of Grand Bahama Island. There's a ten-mile-long barrier reef about a mile off this shore and the chart warns of breaking waves in many places. The guide book lists three marinas inshore behind the reef and each must have some sort of entrance-channel through the reef.

Since Lucayan Marina is the only one with a buoy marking its hole through the coral, it looks like the best bet and the Wests are to meet us there. But this piloting info seems much too sketchy and unreliable. With the marinas so far in from the reef we won't be able to distinguish details as we sail along outside the reef. How, we wonder, is one supposed to find a hole in a submerged reef except by spotting that one marker? And, after dead reckoning for six hours and making landfall, how will we know whether to turn left or right to find this "small, cone-shaped buoy"? Surely we'll meet someone at one of our island stops who can fill us in with local knowledge.

SATURDAY, MARCH 17: We're on our way to Highborne Cay by 8:30, sailing out of the eastern end of the harbor among a number of small islands where there are coral heads just below the surface. To be sure that we don't run into one of them, we followed the *Bahamas Guide* instructions, staying close to the north shore as we left the harbor heading for the Narrows, a rusty navigation marker; then to 132° until Ft. Montague and the southernmost span of the bridge were in range behind us. Passed Porgie Rock and turned to 102° at 9:40. We'll hold this course until the eastern-most of two clumps of casuarina trees on long, skinny Rose Island bears 0.0° where it is safe to turn due south on course to Highborne. A few minutes ago a large, dark, round smudge appeared in the water just a few yards to port...so, that's what a coral head looks like! We're also working hard learning how to read the water depths by color, and I've been using the lead-line to check our guesses. It's a sunny day with some puffy clouds, and the water is a beautiful blue with a light chop obscuring the bottom which is as little as five feet and never more than three fathoms below us.

By 10 AM we make the turn to 180° leaving the islets and shallows behind. The genoa is up and we're scooting right along on a close reach. No land in sight ahead; I don't expect to see anything until two or three o'clock. After about twenty minutes I turn around to look aft at low Rose Island beginning to fade in the distance and I notice that just to the right of the second casuarina clump there is what looks like a tiny gap in the island and it is precisely astern when I'm right on 180°. This will be helpful when we return and are looking at a long, slightly ragged, but very thin line of islands on the horizon, miles away, with no other landmarks to indicate where we must make that crucial left turn back to Porgie Rock.

It seems that this is "piloting" in the Bahamas: since the guide books consist of courses, bearings, landmarks and sketches of distant shores but almost no water depths, one must rely heavily on the former while reading the water's colors for depths. Navigation markers, substituting for buoys, typically are no more than a thin, rusty pipe sticking up perhaps ten feet above the water topped with a reflector or light not much bigger than the diameter of the pipe. No numbers or names. We have been told that many of the lights don't work. Our chart of the area has only a few depths, but *does* indicate that up ahead there are two large areas—several square miles—of coral heads labeled White Bank and Yellow Bank which we'll come to in about two hours. Some of the heads could rise to less than four feet below the surface so one of us will have to go forward to the bow to keep an eye out. Our course is supposed to take us between these "nests" where the heads are fewer.

Right on schedule one appears, and then another and another, so Ginger goes forward and I ease the sails way out until the jib luffs in order to slow down. We think we see others just a few yards to one side or the other but the dark smudges are indistinct, and tend to be hidden by the flicker of the waves. Then there are no more for nearly ten minutes. Suddenly Ginger shouts, points, and I veer off. I watch it as it passes close-by to windward; it must be near the surface as it appears not as a smudge but as a clearly defined, black column perhaps six feet in diameter. We're learning. When one looks truly black and hard-edged, it's about four feet down. In another ten minutes we are beyond them and I note the time in the log for our return trip.

At three o'clock we see the first slight hump on the horizon and soon another dead ahead: Ship Channel and Highborne Cays. The latter, Kline's *Guide* says, has quite a high hill, and near its top there should be a small white house. Sure enough, in about a half hour the house appears. I've made a sketch of Highborne in the *Guide* as it appears from four miles out because it's very different from the sketch shown. Now we have to find more landmarks, follow courses and the water's colors as we make our way among several outlying islets and avoid shallow areas while we close on the wharf and size up the anchorage area.

The wharf protrudes from the end of a narrow road running straight up the hill which is densely covered by gray-green, scrub bushes almost hiding several houses near the top. Two sailing yachts are berthed at the far side of the pier and beyond them is barely space for one or two more boats to anchor in that end of the bay. To our right several hundred yards of pure-white beach arc along the shore, and half a dozen, large sailboats are anchored off. We pull in to the pier to learn whatever we can from whomever might be in attendance. Harold Albury appears from the harbormaster's hut to ask if we need fuel, and as we are topping off (less than three gallons), he, like the mayor of a small town, fills us in with all there is to know about the cay. He points out that, with our shallow three-and-a-half foot draft, we should be able to anchor inshore from all the other boats and thus be comfortably clear of the persistent roll in that side of the bay. Following his suggestion Ginger guides the boat along the shore as I heave the lead and find almost five feet no more than 50 yards from the beach and well clear of the other sailboats, all of which are considerably larger than *Lyla*.

By sunset we were settled in and having a comfortable drink in the cockpit…A hale from one of the other sailboats (with hands cupped around mouth), "What type of boat is that?"

"It *was a Swiftsure*," I answered.

After we'd finished our drinks we got in the dinghy to mosey among the anchored fleet. Of course we passed by the man who'd hailed us; he stood at the rail to say, "Very pretty vessel!" Turned out this was Norris Hoyt—a famous *Yachting* magazine author and his wife, Kitty aboard

Telltale. In the ensuing conversation I said something that indicated that I'd read Bill Snaith's books, and we were IN. "Come aboard and tell us about your rebuilding job—she's beautiful!" The moon was up almost as high as my self-esteem before we rowed back to *Lyla*.

The next morning we walked up the steep road to the ridge, past some small houses eave-deep in the scrub growth. Didn't quite get to the "store" which later we heard is almost a joke, and very expensive. The view below to the harbor, the little islets, the sweep of the white beach, the turquoise-and-blue water, Norman's Cay in the distance was right out of a travel brochure. After lunch on board and an hour of maintenance jobs we swam in to that perfect little beach and walked barefoot to its end and back.

MONDAY, MARCH 19: Time to sail back to Nassau and head toward Grand Bahama Island to meet the Wests. To do this we will sail through one of the five island groups of the Bahamas; the Berry Islands, before we can head for Grand Bahama. It will take us about five hours to cross the deep and wide Northeast Providence Channel and make landfall at Whale Cay which is only a few miles from Chub Cay at the southern end of the Berrys.

By the time we'd arrived back in Nassau we were beginning to feel more comfortable with Bahama navigation; certainly it is a new ball game. Courses and landmarks in Kline's *Guide* are helpful but can't always be trusted as are those in the U.S.A.

We were thankful for the notes we took on our way out from Nassau. The "gap" in Rose Island held us on course for many miles and put us right on the necessary spot to make the turn to the west. If we'd accepted the next guide book course past Porgie Rock, it might have put us aground. After adjusting to avoid this, we entered Nassau's harbor and found an acceptable place to anchor for the night close to our departure point for the Berrys.

TUESDAY, MARCH 20: Departed Nassau 10:20 AM and at 3:30 PM, land ho! Whale Cay's protruding, eighty-foot high, central elbow appeared with a dense clump of casuarinas hiding an old, gray, wooden church. The wind on this cloudy, hazy day was at least 18 knots but *Lyla* was in her element, handling the six- or eight-foot ocean rollers with ease. Our location confirmed by the church, we bore off to starboard to Whale Cay's neighbor, *Little* Whale Cay, looking for a small stone tower leading to an anchorage where we could snug down for the night. The tower turned out to be a new, much higher one of white sandstone blocks which nearly matched the sandstone cliffs behind it. Not like the picture in the guide book at all. It must be the right one though. Nothing else around.

Big, white breakers were crashing against the rocky shores, reverberating back out and producing short, steep, but smaller seas. We headed up just long enough to drop the jib and quickly secure it to the lifeline, a messy job using both hands, feet, knees, and teeth on the plunging foredeck. It was still flogging until Ginger, back in the cockpit on the helm, managed to tame its clew by winching the sheet in tight and cleating it. Too rough out there to let down and furl the main. We edged into the narrow channel between Whale and Little Whale with Ginger up forward at the bow reading the water as soon as we were beyond those seas. Shallow sand bars left and right, some we could see, others were indicated on the sketch-chart as we bore to port behind Whale toward what looked like shelter from the SE wind.

The rather high shore, less than a hundred yards away kept the water flat but the gusty wind was scuffing up white-caps big enough to make handling tricky when I tried to slow down. I grabbed the leadline and managed two soundings as I steered the boat in a circle with one knee. Ginger dropped one anchor temporarily to hold the bow into the wind while we lowered and furled the heavy main. Then we set both anchors to hold us in the circle's center where we knew the water was deep enough. One sounding was only about four feet leaving only six inches under our keel, but it was dead low tide. Welcome to the Berrys! The wind would shake the mast violently periodically and we were rolling enough to be annoying. But after supper the wind veered to the south, lessening the roll, and down below the noise of waves and wind was muted so we slept fairly well.

The Berry Islands form a small, twenty-five-mile-long, crescent-shaped archipelago about 25 nautical miles NNW of Nassau and 65 miles SSE of Grand Bahama Island. The islands at each end are the largest; Chub is two and a half by half a mile, Great Harbor Cay, at the north end, is five by as much as a mile wide, while the other dozen or so are long, skinny cays often less than a few hundred yards wide, uninhabited or sporting a single small settlement. One or two are some wealthy American's hideaway with private air strip and tiny, fairytale beach.

Oriented south to north and unapproachable from the west by many miles of shallow, shifting sandbars, the feeling of isolation pervades this crescent of cays and rocks. The wind is incessant, pushing white foaming breakers into vertical limestone shorelines along the windward east coast. The water is deep blue turning to various shades of turquoise as it shoals between cays and flows into a number of calmer anchorages and small harbors behind their back, or leeward, sides. The currents can be fierce in most of these anchorages it seems, requiring exploration and trial and error before settling in for a night. Did I say "settling"? Typically, after psyching out the currents, discovering a spot where the boat stops jilling around and getting the anchors down, the boat begins to roll! Only a small swell may appear to be the cause, but mysteriously, each roll is more severe than the previous one. After five rolls, the fifth being violent, it stops…Ahhh! The boat is perfectly still for a whole minute, and then it starts all over again. The fourth roll sends coffee cups skidding against the table-fiddle. The heavy boom overhead slams from port to starboard and back despite any lashing one can devise! And the fifth roll is worse! No one could sleep to this. Up come the anchors and one tries another spot.

Visually, these little isles are beautiful. Some are low and covered with gray-green scrub; most have a central spine rising to as much as forty feet including a dense forest of stunted trees. Here and there are clumps of taller casuarinas. As we navigated along cliffy, windward shores we would come to a long, very thin, sand beach, or a beach of cobbles, or a huge rock, or a big, bleached log. No signs whatever of man's presence except for an occasional, lone house almost hidden among the trees. Notwithstanding the foregoing list of dilemmas and the need to be constantly wary, we enjoyed the Berrys.

Incidentally, we've finally become pretty good with the lead-line for reliable soundings in water less than twelve feet. Deeper than this there's too much line to re-coil and heave again rapidly, so the depth-sounder is better. One must swing the lead out ahead of the bow far enough to allow the lead to sink to the bottom before the boat catches up to where it has landed. Then the line must be jerked up taut and vertical as you read the marks on it. A lead lighter than five pounds won't sink fast enough, and won't stay on the bottom when the line is jerked. A cupped, bottom-end filled with Wolf's Head water-pump grease brings up a bottom sample.

It was five o'clock after a day of rousing good sailing before we made it to Great Harbor Cay where we intended to sneak in behind again for the night. The gap between Great Harbor and Great Stirrup Cay with its big lighthouse is quite wide and two sailboats were anchored just in this lee, the first boats we've seen since leaving Nassau. We continued on into Panton Cove where the chart shows a small, round islet near the high hill on which Great Stirrup lighthouse is perched. The water shoaled to five feet but we kept going several hundred yards farther, heading for a spot between the islet and the shore which looked very sheltered. Sure enough the wind ceased, enabling us to go slowly, lead-lining our way over four-foot places, and finally finding five feet again directly below the lighthouse. Two anchors down in firm mud. Perfect!

At six, the next morning we set off northward for Grand Bahama and Lucayan Marina on its south shore 65 nautical miles away. The guide book and the chart showed the buoy marking Lucayan's entrance channel through the reef. There was also a pencil sketch of the buoy and the landmarks on shore as viewed from two miles out. But this sketch gave little confidence in what we'd actually find, especially since we'd learned that Bahama's navigation marks can be very unreliable and even be missing altogether. Approaching the island, we'd plotted a course purposely more than a mile to the left of where the sketch showed the buoy, so we would know surely that we must turn *right* to come to it.

At about two o'clock, with Grand Bahama a long, dark shape on the horizon but yet too far away to discern details, we began calling the marina. Eventually we were answered by *TNT Two*. A Bahamian voice said, "Lucayan Inn, Xanadu Marina and Running Mon Marina all closed…Lucayan Marina only open, mon."

"What facilities at Lucayan?" I asked.

"Don't know, mon. Dhey s'pose have gahs."

"Is there a buoy at Bell Channel reef opening?"

"Yes, mon, s'pose ta be."

Great!…Over an hour later the reef became obvious with its stretches of small, white, breaking waves, and we made our right turn to sail along near it. Buildings, water tanks and various towers on shore were distinct in our field glass. But they didn't match the sketch very well. Slowly we began to pick out pertinent details. A long building with three distinctive pyramid roofs, a high-rise with a curved face, what looked like an indoor sports arena with a big tower on its right, but, among other confusions, the sketch showed the tower on its left! If that buoy doesn't show up, our only alternative is to turn around and proceed west for two hours to huge Freeport Harbor, which is loaded with industry, big tankers and cruise liners. It would be heavily polluted, noisy and no fun at all, plus finding the Wests would not be easy.

So we edged closer to the reef and concentrated on spotting that buoy if it was to be there at all. Taking turns looking through the glass we agreed that there appeared to be two stubby breakwaters on the shore (almost two miles away). Perhaps that's our channel. The chart noted a course of 340° from the buoy to a pair of red and green markers near shore so we slowed down as we approached that bearing to the breakwaters. And there, so small that we almost missed it, was a tiny buoy consisting of two vertical, crossed boards with a plywood disk on top not more than 18 inches in diameter nor more than three feet high. The sketch showed a sharp-pointed nun-buoy. Hah! We made a 270° turn and headed past this thing on 340°, holding our breath as we crossed the line of the reef. After a few minutes we hadn't hit anything, and yes, those were breakwaters ahead and a narrow entrance cut through rising ground.

Once inside, on our left we passed what looked like a long, three-story motel, but the grass hadn't been cut for months. The channel then opened out to a fuel dock ahead and some marina slips to starboard. We fueled up and were told to take any slip. The attendant had a canned smile and a cheeky tone so we didn't ask many questions. We'd learn the ropes from the boats in the slips.

Rounding the corner, the marina appeared as quite large. But only a dozen sailboats, and several big sport-fishermen were tied up to the concrete wharfs and slips. The slip edges were protected with heavy wooden boards but many of these were split, splintered or missing, leaving bent, rusty bolts sticking out of the concrete. There were dozens of empty slips and as we went about choosing one without a boat on either side, we saw that even the concrete was crumbling away. We're prepared for rough slips so we rigged our heavy fender-board outboard of our big fenders to protect our topsides and slid into the cleanest-looking slip. After a little rest we locked up the boat and went exploring.

Immediately we realized that Lucayan Marina *once* had all the elements of a fine resort. Three big swimming pools now were empty. Adjoining each was a deserted bar boarded up with plywood. Nearby was a row of what must have been expensive shops, we learned, by peeking through a broken window. Big men's and women's baths were still open but their nice tile showers were brown with dirt and missing some faucet handles. Outside the marina fence, on the main road, we discovered a new laundromat next to a 7-Eleven-like store, a sad substitute for the sizable but closed market inside the fence. Up on a little knoll was the impressive clubhouse and its huge dining room that *had* had continuous plate-glass windows under broad overhangs all along three sides. We struck up a conversation with the old security guard at the gate asking "What happened here?"

He said, "Ohh, mon…is all so sad, what used ta be wit da British!"

Three days later, just about lunch time, the Wests arrived and as experienced sailors they stowed their gear in a few minutes so most of the afternoon was spent sitting in the cockpit relaxing and catching up with each other. The main feature of their trip is to be the crossing of the Gulf Stream on our way back to the U.S. We'll head for West Palm Beach where it'll be easy for them to catch their plane back to Boston, but it'll be a rough sail. Since there seemed to be little of interest to do at this marina, and since none of us cared to go into the gambling city of Freeport, we decided to shove off about nine in the evening. The wind tends to be lighter at night.

Pat and I went below to plot our courses on the chart. We'll make our way west along the Grand Bahama coast, but once we leave the bank and hit the Gulf Stream current, we will face a sailor's dilemma. We'd like to sail WNW but the current would sweep us way, way north of Palm Beach. When we prevent that by choosing a course to port, on starboard tack, we'd point directly into the southwest wind so now we must turn even further to port until the sails fill out, and then we'd be pushing directly into the Gulf current and making very little headway toward the Florida coast.

Well, Pat, the old sea dog, was never one to shrink from a long thrash to windward when there was no other way. In five hours we were well off the elbow of Grand Bahama with the current pushing us north, but also we were making good progress toward Florida. About one in the morning I decided to tack and face the current because we were being set *too* far north. It took us seven hours to cover less than 14 miles, and not a mile toward Florida, pounding into quite heavy seas—the Gulf Stream humps up in surprisingly little wind. No one got much sleep. Isabelle said she dozed quite well in our one good sea-berth but Ginger kept rolling to the edge of her wide berth. When she went to rouse Pat for his turn on the helm, he was snoring away in a leaping, *forward* berth!

By 7 AM Pat and I were both in the cockpit, a bit stiff with fatigue and a bit cold. Not saying anything, just sailing the plunging boat with its port rail six inches out of the water. In spite of the seas the autopilot was taking the tedium and strain out of keeping the boat on course, but every few minutes it would get confused when an extra-large wave slapped the bow. I'd have to prevent it from sending us way off in a new direction and help it settle down again. The ladies were stirring below, having given up on sleep. Pat and I began getting whiffs of something cooking. Soon, Ginger was handing up heavy mugs of spaghetti soup, thick, hot and rich. Bravo! Just after noon we spotted the tip of the highest, high-rise condo building on the horizon just north of Lake Worth Inlet. We calculated that it was 18 miles west and already slightly south of us. Nothing to do but sail right in to shore, then tack south hugging the beach to get out of the current for more hours to reach the inlet.

The sun had set when we made it through to the Intracoastal. By the time we reached Riviera Beach Marina it was dark and spitting rain. The fuel dock's bright floodlights revealed several large boats, part substance and part black shadows, crowding each end of the fuel dock, and the wind was gusting over twenty-five knots. We'd have to slide into the space between these boats and stop abruptly before we hit one of them. Pat exclaimed, "D'you think you can get in there?"

Without taking my eyes off the scene ahead, I said, "Wrap a springline one turn on the winch, hand it to me and get ready to jump off with the other end—I got it nailed!" With full reverse roaring, *Lyla* stopped dead for just a moment alongside, and not a lot more than a foot from the dock. Pat jumped off, striding upwind to slip the line's big eye over a cleat well forward as the bow began immediately to swing out and the boat to drift away. A little reverse throttle, another turn around the winch, and *Lyla* nestled against her fenders alongside. I felt pretty good about that one as I headed down the dock to call customs.

MONDAY, MARCH 26: The wind is down, the sun is up; a nice day coming up. First order of business is to clear customs. They were closed last night, of course. I had to answer a lot of questions before the officer was convinced that we hadn't imported a boatload of drugs. After breakfast, the Wests got ready to leave and I hiked off to a telephone booth to call a rented car for them to drive to the airport. Sorry to see them go. It's been great to sail with close friends.

Ginger and I got underway to nearby Florida Diesel, a Universal Engine dealer where I can pick up some spare parts, and I wanted them to check an erratic alternator that has been getting worse. Nice people with a large engine facility wedged into the industrial part of West Palm's waterfront. Every inch of floor-space is utilized, and every square foot of water has a boat in it. Ginger made use of a laundromat down the street and I went along towing our two folding carts to transport groceries from a Pantry Pride only another two blocks away. Then we headed south down the waterway to an anchoring spot next to the Palm Beach golf course. This is right in the middle of Palm Beach but there's a sheltering clump of casuarinas and no noisy traffic. Palm beach tries to be *so* spiffy while West Palm is a typical American city. It's okay...

By the next day the wind had changed forcing *Lyla* close to a lee shore so we moved across the waterway to a small bight next to TV Channel 5, which turned out to be nicer than expected. It was occupied by only one boat, a pretty, 30-foot sloop owned by John Ottman.

Here there is good shelter provided by trees and tall buildings from S by W through N winds. Holding is excellent. A small, quiet park separates the cove from city traffic and there's even a tiny beach just big enough to land a dinghy, haul it up on the grass and chain it to a big tree out of sight from sidewalks. John told us there was even a water faucet behind the trash enclosure, and a phone and block ice at the nearby marina. One could spend weeks here! A block from Channel Five's building we walked across the bridge to explore among the big-name boutiques of Palm Beach, and wandered into the old Flagler Hotel. It was reassuring to see that it still holds up its high class with proud reserve.

SATURDAY, MARCH 31: Grudgingly we've realized that its time to be heading north. We're due home in a month as Ginger has B&B guests scheduled to arrive on May 3rd. As we turn around and head back up the waterway, life will be a little easier since we will not be dealing with unknown territory every day. We have firm ideas about places we don't ever want to be caught in again and many more which we look forward to exploring further. Today we'll make it to Manatee Pocket and Monday we'll pull in to anchor near the nice, city dock at Vero Beach; the next night at Cocoa Beach and then Titusville. It should all be easy sailing.

WEDNESDAY, APRIL 4TH: We are in the fully-enclosed harbor of Titusville and it has rained almost every night since we left West Palm. Rain is no problem for us, but last night, in Cocoa Beach at a wide-open marina, we were tied alongside a bulkhead in between two big, 45-foot Hunter sloops. When a violent, "wham-und-bammer" thunderstorm came through, these vessels were yawing and bucking wildly against their lines. With their high topsides, light weight, and thin mooring lines, I was afraid those boats might break loose and crash down on us. This morning, which dawned clear and calm, I stepped out on the dock to have a look. Sure enough one of the Hunters' lines was chafed half-through and the boat's thin, fiberglass topside was smashed in from blows against the top of a piling.

Titusville Marina, by contrast, is secure in its own little lake. An orderly and prosperous-looking facility, it includes a boat yard with a well-stocked store. All facilities—laundry, phones, fuel, water, block ice, clean bathrooms—are well maintained, plus there's a secure dinghy landing where one can leave a dinghy without worrying that someone will stop by with a pickup truck and carry it off. A fresh-produce market, a discount supermarket, a Burger king and a Mexican restaurant are only four blocks away. We went off to a movie and, returning after dark, discovered that it had rained quite hard requiring us to execute "the cruising man's dinghy drill." To bail and wipe dry an inflatable on a beach without getting any sand in it—sand would cause the floorboards to wear through the fabric, plus sitting on a very wet surface isn't acceptable—then launch it, get in it, shove off and start the outboard without wet shoes or sandy feet, is an art that must be comical to watch. And remember too, that with any wind, small waves will splash into it given the slightest opportunity. Even without rain, an inflatable is soaked with dew an hour after dark. Back aboard *Lyla*, all seems serene. By the time I'd made fast the anchor light to the forestay, checked the chafing gear on the anchor rodes and watched how our movements synchronize with those of neighboring boats, Ginger has lit the lamps and settled into bed with her book.

About six months ago I solved a long-standing problem. Strangely, I had been unable to find an anchor light which could run all night and not need new batteries every few days. I knew that six double-A cells would fit in the light's case if I taped and soldered them all together. The solution was to replace the socket with one for a 4.5 volt bulb instead of three; this lash-up lasts for months. I'll put up with a half-hour's soldering if it occurs only every three or four months.

During the next ten days we sailed through the northern third of Florida and more than the entire coast of Georgia. Most of this stretch was interesting to experience once but not again. One winds through a seemingly endless morass of rivers and creeks in the marshes. Now and again we'd come upon an immense and beautiful panorama; but up close at five knots, much of this landscape reveals itself as a muddy swamp, certainly remote and vaguely threatening in its remoteness. As a human being, I felt as if I shouldn't be invading this kind of place.

We stopped for lunch at Jekyll Island because its history would surely offer a distinct contrast. In the late 1800's, the Rockefellers,

Morgans, Vanderbilts, and others of like ilk, built summer "cottages" there. Near these sumptuous houses a huge clubhouse was built. Originally designed by a Chicago architect, it has been beautifully restored, and in the intervening years the oaks have grown to be truly magnificent. We sat on a stone bench under their spreading branches having our picnic and enjoying the whole scene. Afterward, as we walked around the clubhouse admiring the details of its design, a caretaker approached us and we struck up a conversation. I had barely if ever heard of the Jekyll Island Club, but this is what I learned.

The clubhouse was built in 1886 as a place where the big financiers of the time and their families could gather to ride, hunt and relax out of the public eye. The island was stocked with quail, pheasant, turkey and deer complete with a full-time game keeper. An 18-hole golf course was built, and later a second one was added.

As the severe financial crisis of 1907 spiraled into a panic, Nelson Aldrich, then the leading governmental authority on banking systems, called half a dozen top financial brains to a meeting at the club. A private rail car was parked at an unused platform in the station in Washington, D.C. Each man was instructed to arrive there individually, on a certain night, in complete secrecy for the trip south to Jekyll. They were then not allowed off the island until they had conceived a plan to prevent a nationwide depression. This meeting was the impetus behind the creation of the Federal Reserve shortly thereafter.

Avoiding Savanna, we stopped short of it at nice, small, Thunderbolt Marina. As I was signing in with my Master Card, the owner's wife stared at it, I thought, suspiciously. I asked, "What's the matter?" She replied, "I am Mrs. Henry S. Jones."

Ginger, standing beside me said, "So am I!" We had a good laugh and were treated almost like family.

FRIDAY, APRIL 13: We arrived at Palmetto Bay in Hilton Head. by 2:30 PM and set our anchors in exactly the same spot we had months before. Drinks with the McNaughtons aboard their schooner and dinner with Ginger's cousin Sallie Doughty; then lots of shopping and laundry the next day while we had Sallie's car to carry it all.

In another two days we were in Charleston by early afternoon and decided to carry on to a nice anchoring spot at Isle of Palms. This was a mistake! No sooner had we set off across that wide harbor—the junction of the Ashley and the Cooper rivers—than we noticed a big thunderstorm building up behind the city. In an hour it doubled in size, becoming a towering monster of black, yellow, and bruise-purple clouds. We must make it through the Ben Sawyer Bridge which will open only briefly at five o'clock or we will have to turn back all the way to Ashley Marina. There is no sort of shelter in between.

The last half mile to Ben Sawyer is a narrow channel through the marshes with barely room to turn around at the bridge should it not be open. And then came the rain, in torrents with lashing wind. It took full throttle to hold the bow into each gust. Must have been more than 40 knots. I couldn't see through the dodger's windshield at all, and peering over the dodger's top-edge, forming a tiny slit between it and the bill of my cap, still I could see nothing a hundred feet ahead of the bow. Lightning flashed almost continuously amid sharp bangs of thunder. Suppose there were another boat in this channel! Very likely if the bridge were to open. I held as close to the bank as I dared with the boat so difficult to control. Suddenly the bridge appeared towering in front of me.

It was closed. I heaved the tiller over making a tight circle and starting back down the channel. Now, I don't want to go so far that I miss the opening before I can get back again. I'm counting minutes, trying to watch for traffic, steering the boat, judging my distance from the bank when I could see it in the drenching rain. Four, five minutes—I'm turning back...I'm just established on the reverse course when suddenly, the high, black bow of a big power boat materializes dead ahead. I make a violent turn to the right and it flashes past without a collision. *That* was *so* close! Because of its speed that boat must have come through the bridge! I throttle up to full power and reach for our air-horn. Four, long blasts—the emergency signal. There's the bridge...It's open! I'm struggling to prevent the wind gusts from pushing *Lyla* into the bulwarks on either side. We're through, and the bridge is already coming down. Ohhh. That was a fully structured disaster which all but happened!

Half an hour later the storm was gone and we were snugged down in the quiet pond at Isle of Palms with the perfect shelter of high casuarinas and mangrove trees all around us. The next morning, several crews of workmen ashore were repairing roofs which the storm had torn loose.

THURSDAY, APRIL 19, 1984: The log book says our destination tonight will be "somewhere on the Wacamaw." There are many good anchorages along this river. It's wide and quiet as it meanders through a large forest of pines and tall cypress. High trees stand in water on both banks, and a half-light filters through the branches between the tall, straight trunks. Stopped at Wachesaw Landing and paid the marina owner $5 to drive us to famous Brookgreen Gardens.

Brookgreen is a sort of east coast version of the Huntington Library gardens in Pasadena. In fact it was created by Archer Milton Huntington and his wife in the 1930's for the purpose of exhibiting and preserving the flora and fauna of South Carolina and displaying heroic-style sculptures. It was built on the grounds of a plantation which dated back to the 1700's. Though it's not of the same class as the Huntington, this is an impressive display.

There are sculptures everywhere, four hundred, in fact. Round a corner and a tall, heroic statue may confront you. Walk over to look at a flowering shrub and a small work peeps out through the foliage. Classical, stone pergolas contain whole sculpture collections. The central walk is covered by the wide, overhanging branches of eight enormous and precisely placed southern oaks dripping with beards of moss. As one looks ahead down this long, shaded walk, directly in one's focal point is some small object gleaming in sunlight, far ahead in the next garden. As one enters that garden, it is revealed as a twice-life-size statue of Apollo in gleaming gold.

Shoulder-high walls of ancient, over-fired bricks surround these large, formal gardens. Beyond are a half-dozen acres preserved to look just as they did before Europeans arrived; impenetrable, three-foot high grasses, long, leafy vines and a profusion of low plants choking a tiny creek. It is right at the height of spring here; huge rhododendrons are in full bloom. Every plant, bush and tree is unobtrusively labeled. Too much to take in on one day; we'll be back next year.

WEDNESDAY, APRIL 25: The last five nights in five destinations were uneventful. Most were in places which we looked forward to, such as Seapath, one of our favorites. This afternoon we have arrived at Whittaker Creek in North Carolina, the interim terminus of our '83-'84 cruise. We'll fly home from here and I'll return when it is convenient with three men to help me sail to Norfolk and then directly from Hampton Roads to the Vineyard—380 nautical miles in the open Atlantic.

This marina, as I mentioned before, is owned by Dan Foreman, son of a Vineyard friend. Dan and Bill Lynn run a very organized and complete facility. Ninety-five percent of the boats here are sailboats and it has recently expanded to 150 slips and enlarged its yacht supply store. It has a pleasant lounge, washers and dryers in a neat laundry, good water, propane, kerosene, block ice, charts, telephone booth, barbecue and a courtesy car providing access to a supermarket, a sail-maker and more in the town of Oriental. The piers, sheltered by tall trees, are heavily built with floating slips and outlying piles so that a boat can be tied clear of the finger-piers with four lines and springlines to survive almost any hurricane on its own. The staff prides itself on caring for boats of absentee owners. In addition, Bill's wife Candy commutes to New Bern daily and will deliver or pick up customers at the airport making this an A-1 cruising stop for short or long stays, re-supply, or crew change. We spent a day just relaxing, shopping and attending to various chores, preparing *Lyla* to be left alone and ourselves to fly home. Ginger called our house-renters to alert them and to ask that the telephone be switched back to our number. Funny; this is all a little unsettling. We're certainly not very excited at the prospect. The next morning Candy drove us to the airport and by five o'clock we were in Vineyard Haven. I had just one thought, " Take a deep breath, now; what lies ahead?"

SUNDAY, MAY 12: Back to familiar habits, familiar routines, and to a social life. Back to using the telephone whenever we wished to call a friend or catch up with all that has happened in the last half year. Back to unrestricted land mobility with our own car. Back to work and starting up the furniture manufacturing business again.

The first week was a bit frantic of course, especially with B&B guests arriving a week ago, Friday. In addition to all of the above, we've discovered that re-entering "the real world" is neither automatic nor easy. In fact it's turning out to be a little unsettling. Too many unrelated activities. Too many superficial or boring demands on our time. Too much paper work. Now we fetch a newspaper every day. On the boat we rarely thought of a paper—not being part of the newspaper's world and not having time to read one.

TUESDAY, MAY 28: We've been home almost a month and life is only just now beginning to feel normal. We are back in harness. Though many activities are easier to carry out ashore than aboard *Lyla*, each of these lives has unique pleasures and challenges; each has its own, distinct reality, but which is the real world? A new question: in which do we wish to continue? We never expected that returning ashore would entail this pervasive reentry. Often *Lyla*'s world seems far more rational and free of the inconsequential. Life ashore seems less rational, less rewarding, satisfaction less attainable, the rules less clearly laid out. Is that what we want? Do we now have less control over our lives? Just what sort of control do we want, or need?

Responsibilities ashore are complex. Aboard *Lyla* they're less complex because they're focused solely on sailing the boat and the commitment to the tasks of keeping her functioning and safe. Coupled to that, every day is another adventure. New places to see, new people to meet, new challenges to surmount. A well-designed sailboat, properly sailed, becomes so much more than just a machine.

THURSDAY, MAY 30: Hot dawg! It's time to go fetch *Lyla*. I called three friends today, each a good sailor intrigued with the idea of three days at sea. With their help we will sail directly from Norfolk to Vineyard Haven, and as we pass New York we'll be almost fifty miles out in the Atlantic. The 380 nautical-mile distance, can be sailed in about three days if we don't have to tack in head winds a lot. The same trip "inside" would take at least two weeks.

FRIDAY, JUNE 1: I flew into New Bern, North Carolina today. Candy picked me up at the airport and brought me back to Whittaker Creek in the late afternoon. *Lyla* is just as we left her, lying quietly in her slip. Tomorrow I'll take her over to Sailcraft Boatyard, about a mile away, where she will be hauled for the weekend while I inspect the bottom, paint it, lubricate all the through-hull sea cocks and check them for electrolysis.

SATURDAY, JUNE 2: The haul-out was interesting as it was done completely by one man. Other shipyards that I know, with a similar Travelift, would put two or three on the job. I did have to help him by sliding the straps into the right places along the keel—I have appropriate marks on the waterline; he'd never seen *that* before. He settled *Lyla* down gently on three timbers arranged beforehand, climbed down from his big machine and had four Brownell-stands adjusted to support her in less than ten minutes. This yard hauls for do-it-yourselfers only on weekends so I had Saturday afternoon and Sunday to do the work. Prepped all afternoon, checked and lubed the six sea cocks. The bottom was not bad at all considering that it had been a whole year since the last painting, but it had enough growth on it to slow us down somewhat. I taped the waterline the next morning plus other work. Painted in the late afternoon and she went back in first thing Monday morning—ideal timing for the anti-fouling paint.

By noon Monday I was back in the Whittaker slip so I took the courtesy car to town for groceries and boat supplies. That left Tuesday to get the boat ready for the voyage and the crew before the boys arrived about 4:00 PM. And, oh yes, all the ice the fridge could hold. Spent over an hour explaining to Joe, Travis, and Bud all about *Lyla*'s rig and reefing system, how each sail is set, fitting a safety harness for each man, going over charts. As they settled in below there were dozens more questions—the location of many items, how the watch system would work and what to expect during the three days we'd spend getting to Norfolk. After dark we had dinner ashore barbecuing steaks I'd bought.

Wednesday dawned warm and humid so we were all up early and under way by 7:40. Sailing up the Neuse River to Maw Point is a straight shot, an easy first leg to enhance the boys' learning curve. Then around that point heading for the Pungo River.

We tacked several times with a rising wind providing good practice with this maneuver. Joe suggested that we reef the main as a drill so they would all have experienced it before having to do it out in the Atlantic under possibly stressful conditions—an excellent idea. They tied in a single, first, and then a deep reef, learning to sweat the clew-cringle aft and down to the boom to maintain the sail's shape. The "jiffy-reefing" lines do the heavy work but some hand-tugging results in a shape better than the roller-reefing of my previous boat.

The Alligator-Pungo canal is an unattractive stretch and our first stop just beyond it offered only convenience because Tuckahoe Point is a desolate place. There was really little of interest except sailing *Lyla* and experimenting with the auto-pilot.

The next morning we headed up the widening Alligator River with the southwest wind giving us a nice sail on a broad reach. The boys now have had enough practice to begin working as a team. They've agreed to take the Dismal Swamp route so, as we made our way across the fourteen-mile wide Albemarle, we bore west a little to head into the Pasquotank River.

The ICW offers two routes from here to Norfolk and the Chesapeake, and since I had "done" the North River route, I thought it would be interesting to pass through the Dismal Swamp Canal looking for evidence of its history. Listed in the National Register of Historic Places it's the oldest continuously operating canal in the United States. It was fought over by Union and Confederate forces during the Civil War, and, long before that, George Washington explored the Great Dismal Swamp, deciding in 1763 to have the land surveyed for a canal. He pushed hard for its construction because, at that time, there was no way for passengers or commerce to travel between the Chesapeake area and the big North Carolina Sounds of Albemarle and Pamlico except by the treacherous passage outside in the Atlantic around Cape Hatteras where a dozen or more vessels were being lost every year. Work finally began in 1793 and continued for twelve years under horrible conditions as the slaves of local plantation owners dug the canal by hand.

After several hours the U.S. Navy's enormous blimp hangars rose slowly above the horizon beyond the Pasquotank's western shore. Another hour brought us to a marina near what appeared to be the dammed-up end of the river at Elizabeth City. This marina is in two parts. We could get only ice and water at its first location before having to move on to another dock for gas. There seemed to be little reason to give this outfit any more of our money, so we moved on about fifty yards to tie up at the free, town bulwark. Without a cooling headwind, suddenly the heat of the day hit us. The sun beat down unmercifully, feeling like at least 100° and humid. Bud and Travis decided to go off exploring the town while Joe and I rigged our big awning to keep the sun off the cabin and shade us as we sat in the cockpit open to the slightest breeze. We were mighty glad when the sun sank behind the town's buildings.

FRIDAY, JUNE 8: About a hundred yards from where we were tied up, a narrow opening leads through two bascule bridges to a greatly diminished Pasquotank which twists and turns through woods, fields and swamp for eight miles before suddenly becoming a ruler-straight, narrow, dug channel ending at South Mills Lock, the beginning of the 22-mile-long canal itself. Although it would take only about four hours to sail this distance, the lockmasters at each end are very concerned about controlling the speed of boats, especially power boats whose wakes could do much damage to the historic banks of the canal. Thus they require that any vessel desiring to pass through in one day must enter by 9 AM. We were up pretty early to make it to the lock for this first opening of the day, arriving promptly at 8:55 but the lockmaster kept us waiting—going round in circles—until 9:45 before he let us in to be lifted about 12 feet. When the exit gates opened we were confronted by two walls of dense 50- to 60-foot-high trees crowding impenetrably along each bank of the straight canal which disappeared at some infinite distance ahead. Occasionally there would be a break where the trees thinned out to low bushes and tall grasses. Sometimes the channel would widen but most of it was not much wider than a hundred feet. At places, ancient, low, wooden bulwarks restrained the banks; solid fences of slim tree trunks driven into the mud. How these have survived since George Washington's time is a mystery to me.

Today is hot again but with the aft half of the canopy left in place to shade the cockpit, and some headwind, it's not too bad. About one-thirty we arrived at Deep Creek Lock where there was a bulkhead to tie to; and again, like yesterday, the moment our forward motion ceased we gasped from the heat. When the lockmaster informed us that we'd have a two-hour wait, the boys immediately jumped ship to walk to a drugstore for ice cream. They didn't return until the entire two hours had passed and from the remarks and laughter as they came back aboard I gathered that there were some pretty sporty girls there spicing up the ice cream.

When we were finally cut loose, in only a few minutes we were surrounded by the heavy industry and commercial shipping of Norfolk. First the huge Gilmerton bridges and shortly thereafter the Norfolk & Western and Jordan bridges lined our way to Willoughby Marina which will place us close to Hampton Roads. From there, tomorrow, we will depart out into the Atlantic and set a course toward the Vineyard.

SATURDAY, JUNE 9: Departed at 9:45 AM on a hazy, humid day with light wind, and visibility no more than three miles. We headed NW in a small channel for about a mile before entering the main Hampton Roads channel which we followed eastward to reach the ten-mile-wide mouth of Chesapeake Bay. From there, for ten miles, one sneaks along the southern edge of the mouth, where there's less current, on the way to the southern opening of the Chesapeake Bay Bridge. After passing through it, we had to turn NE directly across the ten-mile throat where, though we were dealing with currents as strong as four knots pushing us sideways, at least these currents were flowing more in the direction we wished to go. While we didn't see any of the big gyres that form randomly in this area, we were constantly surrounded by powerful swirls and long streaks in the water. I have no idea what volume of water must flow in and then out through this throat, twice each day, but it must be stupendous. Eventually we changed course once more, taking advantage of the last hour of outgoing tide as we cleared Cape Charles and turned north in the Atlantic.

Now, can you imagine the discussion and arguments that went on down below in *Lyla* last night for an hour as we figured out the courses and timing through all these currents? For much of the day we used corrections of 20° or more, to compensate. We tried the radio direction finder to take a number of sights but the interference was so great that only one station gave a distinct bearing and we had to give that up. Luckily—or perhaps instead—there was a buoy every few miles, and with the headland of Cape Charles becoming distinct in the distance we were never very concerned about where we were.

By 1700 hours, the sun was an orange ball above the western horizon and we were well settled on a course which we can stick to throughout the night about eight miles off the Maryland coast. A nice breeze of 12 knots filled the sails toward dusk, moving us along smartly on a broad reach. The engine, thankfully, is off! We've begun regular, four-hour watches with one man sleeping, one below and doing the cooking and the third on the helm. I'll sleep or cook when I'm not needed topside; the watch is to wake me if a buoy is missed or there is a big wind shift. The latter would wake me anyway. The autopilot relieves much of the strain on the helmsman such that a four hour stretch is acceptable while his watch-mate can always come up for a sail change or relief if he gets tired.

Running at this distance off shore we can see the larger details on shore and, at night, the looms of the lights of larger towns. In addition we will pass a sea buoy about every 20 miles. The lights on these buoys, though small, can be seen almost as far away as a buoy can be seen in daylight—two to three miles. If there is any question about which buoy we are seeing, I've given orders to change course to pass it close enough to read its number for positive identification. This is "coastal piloting" at its most interesting and we use all the little tricks in the book to track our position. Piloting is one of my favorite occupations. Each detail, each light, its bearing and time, the sea and the angle of the swells, the wind on the sails and the character of the weather all form a single, integrated pattern. Any anomaly requires an explanation.

About 2100 hrs: All is in order and I'm ready to get some sleep. Both men on watch have their harnesses on, the wind has been steady and the sails are asleep. The waves are just big enough to form little whitecaps which leave long, phosphorescent trails as each slides down the back of a swell. There's a nice woosh-whishhh as the boat pushes them aside, and down below the angle of heel forms a snug cradle between bunk and hull.

A little before midnight I wake. We should be coming up on "Winter Quarter." I should go back to sleep but I can't get rid of the feeling that I need to spot that buoy. I overhear the helmsman and his watch-mate comment on it but now I'm up anyway. We note the time and check the chart again. Eighteen minutes to go and no buoy flashing out there yet. Ten minutes pass. What the heck! We should see it! Another ten minutes; nothing. "Well, we've passed it by now!" Joe, the helmsman says. Silence. Three of us looking carefully all around.

"Hold your course and keep looking, Joe" I say. The watch changes and after a while we give up and begin to chat quietly. I'm ready to get some more sleep.

As I turn to go below, Bud, who's now on the helm calls, "Hold up a minute, I think I see something."

"Where?"

"Off to starboard fifteen degrees."

A couple of minutes later I say "OK, I see it…four seconds…Yes, I'm counting again; four seconds. It must be four or five miles off station. I'm going below to look at the Coast Pilot." And there it was listed 13 miles from the previous buoy instead of nine. My chart was out of date, but not the book. The Coast Guard *does* move buoys now and then as shoals or other conditions change, and each lighted buoy has a distinct flash-pattern.

We held this course, varying it only a few degrees for tidal changes, for fourteen hours while the wind went more westerly and rose to fifteen or eighteen. Switching to the working jib we were much more comfortable, and with the rail not quite down, our speed increased to seven knots. The sail change went better than I expected with help from a half moon. Two men on a sloping foredeck, their harness-lines clipped to a grab-rail, a loose halyard to transfer to a flogging sail as the latter is clipped to the forestay, and with spray breaking over the bow, this situation invited a tangle. But the new sail went up smartly and *Lyla* regained the speed lost during the change. These sailors race often enough to be handy on the foredeck—only sail-changing in the dark was new to them.

SUNDAY, JUNE 10: Just before midnight we passed the R-2 whistle buoy off Barnegat Inlet halfway up the Jersey coast, and by mid morning we were crossing the traffic lanes for big ships heading into New York. The day has come up clear with only a few little clouds, but the wind has dropped so the engine has been started to help us along.

At 0940, the orange-white whistle which marks the line between the incoming and outgoing New York traffic lanes appears, and we change course a bit to track east of Montauk point as we head toward Block Island a mere eighty miles away. Way up ahead there is some boat right on our course. It appears to be sitting still, and as we get closer, I can see through the glass that it's a Coast Guard vessel. We veer off a little to pass him and as we do so he hails us through a powerful loudspeaker, "Sailing vessel, head up and prepare to be boarded."

"What is this?!" Joe exclaims, "Some kind of inspection?...Way out here, thirty miles from land and forty from New York?"

Promptly the Coast Guarders put over an inflatable launch. Three men jump in and head toward us. As they come along side I start to go forward to take their bow line; one of them barks "Belay that. All on board stand for inspection!" They're all armed and one holds a rifle; this looks serious! They pile on board and step into the cockpit along with three of us which is awkwardly comical because there's not room for that many. One of them heads below carrying some sort of tool which he proceeds to jam into the head after which he begins to search every locker and drawer. It's obvious they are looking for drugs. I'm really scared because I've heard recent stories of the Coast Guard tearing out, with a crow-bar, all the cabinetry in a sailboat. Out in the cockpit the other two search each of us and the captain asks the standard question, "Where's the life jackets?" Opening the seat locker I show them to him and he carefully counts them—there's six and only four of us—nothing wrong with that!

Suddenly they seemed disappointed and unsure what to do next. The captain said, "Don't any of you move. I'm going below to write this up and the master of this vessel will sign it."

It took a long fifteen minutes before he climbed back into the cockpit, gave me the form to sign and handed me a copy as I asked, "Did you find anything wrong?"

He said, "You may read the report." Therewith they climbed back into their launch and sped off. The four of us sat quietly in the cockpit nonplused by the weaponry they carried and the threat they emitted.

With the wind still light out of the southwest we set the genoa again and got underway. The Long Island shore became visible in the distance and, as the hours passed and we slowly closed with it, we began to pick out familiar landmarks realizing that we are in familiar waters and that this voyage will soon be over. As we approached the East Hampton shore during the night the wind dropped to zero so we ran the engine for an hour when abruptly with a puff, and then another puff, the wind came in suddenly from the NNE. After days of running free, with southwest and west winds behind us, now we are close-hauled, "hard on the wind," and will continue to be after we tack to the north around Block Island just after midnight. Then one last long tack all the way to the Vineyard. We expect to be home by mid-afternoon.

Chapter Two
Busy summers on the Vineyard

FRIDAY, JUNE 15, 1985: Summer is in full swing with most of our summer friends now in residence. Ginger is fully occupied with B&B activity and I'm busy with the two young cabinetmakers I'd hired last summer working with the short-run production setups I'd created to manufacture six casual furniture products in runs of a hundred each. U.P.S. appears every few days to pick up finished, packaged and sold items. Last night I relaxed by leafing through *Lyla's* log book. On the page after the conclusion of our voyage are the following notes:

> On the summer weekends of 1984 we raced occasionally with the Holmes Hole Sailing Association. But more often we ran the race committee using a friend's big motorsailer or *Lyla* as a committee boat. During the week I was fully occupied with The Woodworks, a business that continued through the winter and into the present year of 1985. It kept me too busy to do much else, however I did manage to install refrigeration on *Lyla*, and make a longer tiller from some 400-year-old English oak. Also, I installed a Raytheon Loran navigation system, and bought two folding bikes.

In 1985 Loran prices became affordable for the first time, and the sets now read out Lat/Long directly, obviating the former, painful, manual, calculation from time-differences. This will make off-shore cruising and mucking about in the outer Bahamas more precise and less risky. Finally, also, I learned how to adjust the auto pilot so that it became a faithful friend and will eliminate one crew member from multi-day offshore trips out of sight of land.

Last September, as we have for the previous eight years, we were involved with the George M. Moffett Race which is held just before

Labor Day and is open to any single-hull sailboat between 16 and 60 feet in length. It attracts traditional and modern, cruising and racing types, all fifty or so boats racing together in one class under a handicapping rule adapted especially for this race. There are always at least half a dozen big schooners and many smaller gaff-riggers such as a New York 40. Then there are Solings and Cal boats, many cruising classes, even a Rhodes 19, et cetera. Old hands would say that handicapping this disparate assembly is impossible but with the experience of five experts, each versed in one of the types, there have been few complaints through the years this twenty-odd mile race has been run. I'm the junior, sixth-wheel of this group, so it's my job to gather the entrants' specifications, run the handicap numbers and listen to the experts argue about them. They succeed partly because one of the five has watched each of about 90% of entrants perform in many other races for years.

Three of these experts will be on the committee boat as I, with a team, run the starting sequence flags, the time-clock and set the finish-line while they call out any rule infractions or penalties. Ginger would be on board too but she has to manage the setup on our front lawn for the after-race party. Two hundred sailors show up for beer, wine, clam chowder and trophy awards. As part of the preparation, she will have several strong helpers carry an abandoned, wooden dinghy up from the beach to our lawn where it will be turned upright and filled with cases and cases of beer and dozens of wine bottles all smothered in crushed ice. Parking for two hundred people on our dead-end street? Never a problem—they all row their dinghies in to the beach and walk through the woods up to the lawn. Many of the contestants come every year from a hundred miles around and may see each other only this once in the season. For just a moment, if you give your imagination free reign, you *might* catch the spirit of this crowd.

Far into the night, long after we've gone to bed…listen: out in the harbor the party's still going on!

Strangely, as fall crept up on us—and we got through another successful Moffett Race—I don't remember any discussion about going south again. I think both of us felt that there was unfinished business and that of course we'd go. However, this second trip will be different right from the start. Tomorrow I'll begin by asking two or three men to help me sail *Lyla* directly to Atlantic Yacht Basin south of Norfolk. That will save three weeks and hopefully shorten our time in cold weather.

In our heads we have lists of places to visit; places that we passed on our first trip and want to explore. And then there are those other places along the waterway which surely we will avoid. Instead of consistently following the waterway we'll undertake some faster passages outside in the Atlantic, including overnights which can cover three times the distance one can cover inside in the ICW. Last year every day was a venture into unknowns. This year we can reduce the unknowns while preserving the adventuring parts. We're more knowledgeable and skilled, and we will be able to plan ahead making choices which we could not last year.

THURSDAY, SEPT. 12: Joe Eldredge, who with his wife, had rented our house two years ago, has agreed to join the crew of two others if they could have the house again so now we're committed. I called Mr. Thomas at NOAA (National Ocean and Atmospheric Administration) for a long-range forecast. He predicted several days of north winds beginning Tuesday or Wednesday; thus we sail next week.

Chapter Three
A long thrash to windward
ccccccccccccccccccccccccccccccccccccccccccccccccc

WEDNESDAY MORNING, SEPT. 18: By 10:30 we were on our way in a gentle breeze out of the southwest. As soon as we'd rounded West Chop we were close-hauled with the big genny strapped down. The engine was on to help us along down Vineyard Sound's north shore where, as close to it as we dared, there should be little foul current. Managed to get just beyond Tarpaulin Cove on Naushon Island before we had to tack back across the Sound followed by another two tacks to clear Gay Head on a long leg south toward the Vineyard Sound whistle buoy—known as the *Moaner* for its wave-generated, mournful sound. The seas from Gay Head to the Morse A whistle east of Block Island were building up as the wind increased, and just at sunset we ducked behind a long tow—meaning a big, sea-going tug pulling a huge barge on a three hundred-foot-long cable. In the failing light this looked like two separate vessels with our bow aimed right at the space between. We knew better and ducked astern of it. There's four of us on board, Michael, Joe and Roger.

WEDNESDAY EVENING, 2130 hrs: The wind has picked up to almost 20, we've changed headsails to the working jib and the engine is still on, running at a moderate rate as it adds another knot or two. Tacked repeatedly all night trying to get south of Block before we could turn west. All this tacking greatly increases the distance sailed to get to where we want to go, and no one got much sleep as *Lyla* pitched and tossed into head seas. It would be so much easier if we could just follow a line on the chart between where we are now and a destination, but even a modern sailboat cannot sail much closer to the wind direction than about 45°, thus tacking from close-hauled on one tack, through the eye of the wind to close-hauled on the other, entails changing course about 90°. There's not much talk in the cockpit; the sole subject is, "Where the hell is that Norther?! Are we going to have to tack all the way to Norfolk?"

The seas moderated toward morning and by daylight Thursday we had two-foot seas and wind at twelve knots. But with the wind direction nearly parallel to the Long Island shore there was nothing to be done but continue to tack in and out along that shore. By 0630 we were ten miles SE of Montauk Point, and, at about 1730, having made five more ten-mile tacks, the wind veered westward allowing more comfortable courses which we might be able to stick to through the night. It lasted only two hours before veering 20° this time, almost out of the northwest. "Here it comes," we said, "Come on *baby*, keep swinging north!" For sixteen miles we made much better progress, and with eased sheets, much less strain too. Then, just as we were beginning to think the worst might be over, it backed to southwest putting us "hard on the wind" again. Next it became fluky, teasing us. For more than six hours first it would ease just enough to make sleeping better but in less than a half hour it would switch right back to close-hauled. No sooner would we get the sails adjusted for west wind than it would switch right back to southwest. Toward evening, Thursday, it finally settled into the southwest and increased to twenty knots again as the sea built up to big, long, ten-foot high ocean swells with large whitecaps rolling off their tops. We've just tied in a single reef—better to do it now before dark.

THURSDAY NIGHT, 2230 hrs: A beautiful, clear night with stars visible which I'd never seen before. Now and then we're treated to a glimpse of clouds racing across a half moon. Sleeping is difficult but everyone seems to be getting some rest. The three-stage watch system is working well. I'm up whenever needed which is often because they are new to *Lyla* and two of them are new to round-the-clock sailing. The boat has been doing well under working jib with the rail about eight inches above the water. The seas are too big to use the forward bunks, however the pilot berth is excellent on either tack. In the hours after midnight it became quite chilly; I've introduced the boys to the warmth of a bath towel around the neck and down one's front under the foul-weather jacket.

We've become a team and are somehow enjoying the experience in spite of the high seas which, although less violent than waves the same size near shore, still compel one always to have a grip on something and constantly brace against the boat's motion. Someone remarked, through clenched teeth, "It does help to have gear which all *works*." The auto pilot steers most of the time and saves us much energy. It holds a course almost as well as a good helmsman can and never tires. Occasionally it veers off and the helmsman has to reset it but that is much less tiring than holding a course by a star or by the dim, red, swinging numbers on the compass dial. The Loran tells us where we are but it too must be checked against dead reckoning and occasional sea buoys. There will be no buoys, however, from midnight Thursday to almost noon Saturday. We've decided to put in to Cape May for gas which might run short should all this tacking with the engine running, continue all the way to Norfolk—and we can have a short respite from being tossed around.

SATURDAY MORNING, about noon: We've just spotted the Cape May outer buoy. The Loran seems to be off about three quarters of a mile—not bad! The buoy was easy to see from that distance but we've altered course to read its numbers to be sure it is the right one. The tide between the long entrance breakwaters, and the wind also, will be against us so we don't expect any trouble entering.

We left Cape May at 1330 in twelve knots of southwest wind and made three more tacks. The first was supposed to take us south-by-west along the Maryland coast but the incoming Delaware River current swept us almost to Cape Henlopen. Then a southeast tack has taken us back out to sea to a point where we hope one more tack, parallel to the coast, will let us sail all the way down the Maryland coast through the night. The wind, which backed to south-by-east half an hour ago, has backed to SSE just enough to allow sheets to be eased so we will all get some real sleep at last. (A wind "veers" clockwise and "backs" counterclockwise.)

SUNDAY, SEPT. 22, 0510 hrs: The sun is up but it's very hazy. We've just passed Parramore Banks whistle-buoy and expect to make Hampton roads well before dark if this southeasterly wind holds.

1730 hrs: By noon the sky was overcast, the barometer had dropped and it began to rain an hour ago. The Loran kept us on course while we were trying to pick out the lights of the big, Hampton Roads ship channel. But as we got closer, and just after we picked up some Chesapeake Bay Bridge lights, the Loran went erratic, giving screwy readings just when we needed it to help us find the opening in that long bridge. Switched Loran secondaries which helped only a little. Heavier rain came with the failing light of dusk and we had a nasty thrash against the current, wind abeam, then going aft when we turned into the ship channel. The jib was taken down and stowed to get it out of the way.

Very hard to see anything with the rain now pouring and the wind coming in powerful gusts. Joe and I shared the helm, picking out the channel lights while Mike and Roger stayed dry below locating these buoys on the chart as we shouted numbers or types down to them. We must find and identify the red and green pair of buoys which lead into little Willoughby Channel somewhere off to our left. If we miss them it will be absolute hell to turn around in mid-channel to go back and make the turn-off.

Roger shouts up from below "Willoughby's next, after buoy 28!" There they are, I believe, and I shove the tiller over.

"What's the green's number, Roger? I might be able to see it too." Still raining hard as Joe catches a glimpse of green's number one while I am having trouble wiping water off my glasses with a wet hand and we shoot between the buoys. We had done the right thing when we also furled the main a mile back to obviate a jibe here—took all four of us to do it.

Moving fast in the little channel, we soon passed the big warehouse to port and I started the left turn around the point to the marina, working largely from memory. Suddenly there were docks and boats dead ahead where there should be just open water. Everyone is calling out what he can see. I'm very confused but I stick to my plan as there *must* still be a way through to the marina. A small space appears between a finger-pier on starboard and a big schooner's stern sticking out on port. No more than thirty feet between them! I squeezed through dead slowly, and the space widened out to the familiar gas dock which had been invisible a moment before. Tied up there and explored on foot looking for an empty slip, found one, moved *Lyla* to it, and all hands disappeared to make phone calls!

Mike and Roger left early the next morning as each was several days AWOL from their jobs. Joe and I relaxed over breakfast rehashing the exciting moments of the day before. Making our way out where we had squeezed through last night, we were amazed to see an enormous marina—several hundred boats—where there had been only acres of open, shallow water a year before. Three miles farther along, we passed nearly under the sterns of one of our biggest aircraft carriers, the ocean liner *America* and a mix of Navy cruisers and destroyers. Joe was duly impressed since he'd never been up close to such huge ships. They towered high above us, many times our mast-height. Norfolk Harbor was busy, as usual, with tugs and tows, freighters, dredges and other work boats. The big bridges opened promptly, as did the lock several miles beyond, since now I knew the correct signal. In another hour we pulled into Atlantic Yacht Basin where I'd made arrangements to leave *Lyla* for a month.

Chapter Four
This trip begins with a big cleanup

Ginger, Sasha, the world's most laid-back cat, and I returned on October 22, 1985, after a trip to California and after *Lyla* endured six days of heavy rain produced by Hurricane Isabel. The Yacht Basin's back creek lived up to its reputation as the perfect hurricane hole but *Lyla* sat closed up for this entire period of 100% humidity; the kind of weather about which the locals say, "If you clap your hands, it'll rain underneath them."

We arrived after dark, made our way into the big shed, groping along its barely lit, narrow walkway. I stepped down into *Lyla*'s cockpit, unlocked the companionway, reached in to turn on the main electrical switch and flipped on the galley light—nothing! I tried several other lights. I cycled the main switch repeatedly off and on—nothing. The batteries must be dead! *How* could that *happen?*

We found a flashlight, lit a kerosene lamp, pulled our travel bags down into the cabin, our pillows out of their dry-locker, and climbed into our bunks for some much-needed sleep. Sasha disappeared somewhere in the pitch black cabin but soon hopped up on Ginger's bunk. Now and then he'd sneeze and move around restlessly.

Morning brought a northwest wind and bright sunshine. The stove worked as it uses propane so Ginger soon had breakfast ready. With daylight streaming through our windows, suddenly we saw what had happened. Every surface, wood or fabric, was covered with green or yellow mold including clothes in drawers or in the hanging locker and even on the top two or three charts on their shelf below the settee cushion. The bedspread of each bunk had changed color. Every fabric article on board, except the blankets, bed linens, and towels stowed in the dry-locker, had to be carried to the marina laundry. Everything else, including the inside of every drawer, had to be wiped with a strong

Clorox solution. Our books somehow escaped but they all had to be moved so I could wipe down their shelf. And yes, mold had permeated the vapor-proof main switch which is a heavy, bulky, black plastic affair six inches in diameter. It was removed and set out in the sun. We worked dawn-to-dark for two days. On the third day we shopped. *Lyla* needed everything: gasoline, oil, kerosene, water, propane, and a long list of supermarket items.

Lunched with a very nice couple, Mary and Roger on Satori, eighteen months out of Portland, Oregon. In one way they are typical of longterm live-aboards. They had great stories to tell but then, very complete in themselves, content to be on their way without so much as a so-long.

SATURDAY, OCT. 26, 1985: Departed Atlantic Yacht Basin, 0950, destination wherever along the North River. Nice, sunny day in the seventies. Wind, light easterly. Magnificent mares tails in the sky all afternoon. The radio forecast and the sky foretold a quiet night with the easterly continuing so we selected an anchoring spot on the eastern shore of this broad river. Just above Lutz Creek we left the channel, turning toward a distant group of trees where the water, glassy calm, remained deep right up to the shore. After the anchors were down we sat in the cockpit to watch the sun set, all orange fading to purple, above a two-mile width of gray river, punctuated by a thin, black tree-line defining the horizon. Ginger made great chocolate brownies for my birthday. Dinner was delicious with music and lamp-light.

SUNDAY, OCT. 27: Departed shortly after there was adequate light hoping to get across the Albemarle before the wind rose. In the still of early morning I was able to get both anchors up and stowed, and get underway before Ginger had breakfast ready. Munching granola, I waited a few minutes for sufficient light to pick out the markers when we reached the channel.

MONDAY, OCT. 28: Yesterday's early start enabled us to make it all the way across the Albemarle, down the Alligator, and through the Alligator-Pungo Canal. At its end I'd previously noticed a nifty little cove, so turning right into it I headed for a clump of high trees and found deep water right up to the shore affording shelter from the whole north quadrant. Just before dark an apple-green, forty-eight foot Hereshoff with a long, clipper bow pulled in and anchored near us. We had a nice conversation with Helen and Charlie Reade who are going to Coconut Grove, Florida and then to George Town, Great Exuma, in the central Bahamas. We'll look for each other in harbors along the way.

Today, our destination is our favorite Whittaker Creek. The wind was calm when we started out but began to build when we entered the Pamlico River close-hauled into a fifteen-knot easterly. By noon we'd worked our way into huge, open Pamlico Sound with the wind continuing to increase, and we had a nasty, one-hour thrash around Maw Point—fitting its bad reputation. This is Cape Hatteras, after all, where storms are born. As we swung around into the Neuse River the wind backed into the northeast and we had to run directly down wind. Heavy, tricky, exhausting work steering the boat. I wondered if I could hold out for the ten miles to Oriental. Ginger's just not strong enough to help! When *Lyla*, as a beamy center-boarder, surfs down the back of big, steep swells she wants to veer off to one side or the other requiring a helmsman's full strength against the tiller to keep her going straight ahead. I was *all in* by the time we rounded up into the wind at the Oriental green marker in a boisterous, only partial lee—25 knots and breaking wave-tops all around us—to furl the sails before we could motor through the very narrow channel into Whittaker Creek.

All is calm in this creek, but tonight the wind is shaking the mast over our heads though we're in a slip with dense, tall pines close by. Still much settling in to do. Some things are not yet in their proper places as they've yet to be cleaned of mildew. However, the Clorox odor is gone and *Lyla* smells of teak again.

The trouble with shore-bound life is that its many comforts can breed boredom. In fact one might say comfort has a certain symmetry with boredom. In a safety-circumscribed life ashore many repetitive tasks are done in the name of "comfort." At sea, each of the many tasks is carried out without question because any omission spells trouble ahead and there is a satisfying sense of pride and well-being when all is in order.

Tuesday dawned partly sunny and blow-*ing*. It cleared, then became darkly overcast. The wind came in puffs to 25 or more, then quiet in between. A busy day of groceries, laundry, engine oil-change, new batteries soldered into the anchor light, walking the cat, filling the water tanks, checking courses on the charts, cleaning. Nice to stay mostly below out of the buffeting wind after our rather boisterous sail yesterday. We were very glad to get into Whittaker and also glad we didn't stay back at remote Bay River where we would have been stuck for two days. We saw two boats anchored there as we approached Maw Point and elected to keep going. At the time, I wondered if they knew something I didn't.

WEDNESDAY, OCT. 30: We're off this morning at 8:15 across the Neuse and into Adams Creek without a destination in mind. Ginger didn't much want to stop in Beaufort, so an early start would get us to Peletier or beyond. In spite of foul current we were early at Beaufort so we made a swing through Moorehead City. Along its waterfront were several small restaurants and fish piers, a new condo development with a dozen, empty slips, and a run-down boatyard, all fish-village honky-tonk—no place that we'd want to spend a night. Nothing to do but to move on. Peletier was only a few miles farther, and we would come to it by one in the afternoon, too early to stop there. Twenty miles, or four hours, down Bogue Sound the chart showed a tiny harbor labeled Swansboro Yacht Basin off by itself, nearly a mile from any town. What might we find there? With the word "yacht" in its name it must be a facility catering to vessels larger than outboards, and it might offer some amenities. We'd give it a try. I'd call them on the radio for more information about their entrance channel when we got close enough.

1700 hrs and almost dark: We are in Swansboro Yacht Basin. It is a tight, little hole with a twelve-foot high bank on two adjacent sides. There are three small houses up on the bank, and several larger, dark wood buildings behind a low, wooden fuel dock and dock-house where we are tied up. A dozen or so day-sailer-size slips completely occupy the remainder of the pond. It's absolutely *pouring* rain!

We arrived a half hour ago at dusk, unable to raise anyone on the radio, unable to see well through our wet glasses. In light almost too dim to read the main channel marker numbers we had to find number 45B because it would be the only clue to the location of whatever sort of channel might appear, and then immediately turn right into it. We found that marker's piling and felt our way in until the gas dock suddenly appeared ahead and we managed to tie up to it. No one in sight. Blowing hard, but the water's calm in here. We dove below peeling off dripping foul-weather gear on the way. Changed partly wet shirt, lit the lamps, and the cabin was soon mellow and warm with music and a weather report. Great to have a leak-free boat! Shooting the dock was go-for-broke. No second chance possible. Wow, did it rain! Thundering on the cabin top until 2 am, it then blew violent gusts backing to the northwest, perhaps forty knots at times, shaking and heeling the boat.

Now—thinking back on it again—this was a very risky situation. With no answer to our radio call, we had to *assume* that there must be a channel leading into this place. The chart indicated that there was one near the end of a low bluff along the edge of the main channel, and we were also encouraged by the fact that there was a special buoy there. We'd been following unlighted markers on high pilings, one every mile, so we knew we were getting close when we saw number 44. Twelve minutes later we almost ran into the next pile before we saw it but not its number. I slowed as much as I dared without losing rudder control approaching number 45B but couldn't see its number either. At that moment, about twenty yards off to our right, we both saw the flash of a little red reflector in the water, not much bigger than that on a bicycle, gleaming in our flashlight beam between us and the bluff. I turned sharply toward it, and as we got close, expecting to go aground at any moment, another appeared ahead, and then another, each nailed to a skinny little pole protruding not more than two feet above the roiling water. This channel, likely no more than twenty feet wide, cut right through the bank and, *poof*, like a cork into a bottle, we were in a pond so small that turning around in the high gusts might not be possible, nor did we know whether its edges were shoal. Nothing to do but land at the little dock ahead which will be tricky. High wind-gusts require speed to maintain steering control, while at the same time I must turn and come alongside the dock, hopefully without touching it, and stop the boat abruptly so Ginger can jump off onto it, without slipping and falling, to secure a spring-line.

As I recollect this moment, we're closing with the dock much too rapidly. The rain, splashing on the dark wood of the dock's planks, is reflecting many little highlights from the single spotlight shining down from a big, steel Texaco sign swinging in the wind overhead. The engine roars as I give it full, reverse throttle, and we slide alongside somehow! Ginger drops the spring-line's eye over a cleat and I'm able to spring *Lyla* slowly against the floating dock.

THURSDAY, OCT. 31: Arrived at good old Sea Path about mid-afternoon after an easy day sailing with a north wind behind us. It is a civilized marina. Upon arrival, we asked not to be on the outside transient dock which met with prompt acceptance by the dock master who waved us inside to an available, private slip. We used the courtesy car to shop at the nice mall across the bridge over the ICW. One-hour film service here. Bought fish at Hieronymus Bosch Fish Market, and went to Redix, of course. The old owner was no longer there, and the eclectic stock seemed less appealing.

SATURDAY, NOV. 2: After a day relaxing and sort of hanging out with other sailboat people, we are today on our way through huge Snow's Cut in the sand dune just before it empties into the Cape Fear River. Shortly after noon we stopped to visit old friends on Long Beach Island before continuing on to Lockwood's Folly and a small cove called Blue Point which we managed to get into after dark and in the rain again.

By seven the next morning we were under way and none too soon because coming toward us was the longest tow we've seen yet. We first became aware of it from a steady stream of excited chatter on the radio. Turned the volume up so we could listen from the cockpit. In a few minutes we passed a large tug pulling a very big, clamshell dredge, three hefty work-boats and ten barges, each loaded with 50-foot long dredge-pipes. It all added up to an assembly which must have been a thousand feet long!

The tug captain was faced with maneuvering this unwieldy procession through Lockwood's Folly, a swamp delta near the mouth of a river which empties into the Atlantic. For several square miles this is a maze of wandering interlocking creeks, the deepest of which have been dredged and buoyed to form the winding passage of the ICW. A long train of barges like this will be cutting into the banks at every turn and the morning traffic of perhaps a dozen sail and power pleasure-craft heading in the opposite direction towards him will have to duck into any small irregularities in the waterway's shallow banks hoping to avoid being mashed into the mud by monstrous oncoming barges. We managed to pass them in a short straight space just before the excitement began with all the talk as each vessel made decisions about what to do from what could be learned from the boats ahead, and from the desperate but determined tug captain. Most of the boats would thus learn of this approaching calamity long before they saw it, of course, but they'd be hard-pressed to figure which places would be safe.

Next came the Rock Pile, a twenty-three mile stretch of man-made canal between ten- to twenty-foot high walls cut through solid sandstone. At first it appears to be nothing more dangerous than a gently curving ditch, but just under the water's surface are razor-sharp, dynamited edges of a narrow, central channel so threatening that tugs announce their impending entry and progress on the radio, and we smaller boats also call to learn just when and how they will pass us. Four hours of possibly tense encounters.

By evening, life improved; we'd entered the lovely Wacamaw River, placid and deep to its banks as it meanders among stately old southern cypress and pines. Pulled into Prince Creek where the trees almost close overhead and slowly worked our way in until we found a place wide enough to swing at anchor. Dropped our anchors with buoys attached as the bottom is full of rotting "snags." The weather had been threatening all day and no sooner were we settled than the heavens opened with torrents of rain. How nice it held off until just as I was heading below. Great big drops thumping on the cabin top. No other boats here, perhaps because of the encounter with the long tow. We hoped no one was hurt or boats lost.

THURSDAY, NOV. 7: Another early start and fair current enabled us to make it through the Ben Sawyer Bridge before its restricted period, early enough to get across choppy Charleston Harbor and into Ashley's Marina before dark. New management seems to be keeping up the place better and the attendants are helpful. Notes from the log: "Ice, a few old charts and soft drinks at the office. Propane next door at the municipal marina, kerosene at the Gulf station half a mile to the left."

We set up the bikes for a ride across town to the excellent, big market instead of waiting 15 or 20 minutes for a Dash Bus. We had a fine ride, once we got away from the high speed highway, pedaling nearly four miles through the lower, pretty part of the city among fine old antebellum houses. They're more interesting outside than inside.

Decided to skip the next part of the ICW and make the 40-mile trip to Hilton Head outside so we left Charleston by traveling down harbor for an hour in the evening and over-nighting beyond Fort Sumter in a small bight near the harbor's mouth. It is low and open to wind, perhaps eight feet high at most, but the dunes are high enough to create calm water and we spent an easy night. Upon leaving Friday morning and rejoining the main shipping channel, we were surprised to discover the range markers were steel, openwork towers thirty feet high. All the other marks were easy to pick out and we found the hole for small craft in the three-mile long breakwater to be much more obvious than it looked on the chart. It was a rather bleak-looking morning, chilly, and blowing; the kind of day that a weekend sailor would think, "not worth going out today."

Set a course with the Loran about a mile offshore and settled down to just sailing. There'll be a buoy ahead in an hour. Before long the Loran indicates that the tide is setting us inshore so I enter the buoy as a waypoint and tell the Loran to set the course to it thus compensating for the tide and keeping us off some shallows almost two miles from shore. Had a nice sail; nothing difficult about sailing down this coast outside. The various river mouths are easy to see and we made very good time, so much so that we were able to pass Skull Creek by 4:15 and continue to Palmetto Bay. Ran the engine at a quiet 1250 rpm to keep us really pushing along and get us there before dark. Found all the entrance buoys per chart in Port Royal Sound. Had fair current coming in, however it turned foul on schedule in Skull Creek, and by the time we reached Broad Creek it had slowed us so much that it was long after dark before we dropped the hooks. I could see what I needed to see: black marsh edges, long shimmers across the water from distant house lights, transitory shadows of anchored boats, and a few landmarks I recognized. It would not have been this easy if it had been strange to me. There was Tom's old schooner just where it had been two years before, and also a small sloop called a Virtue.

Got out the bikes on Saturday and found the trip to Wynn Dixie very easy. The saddle bags on the bikes worked only *fairly* well—two big grocery bags on one bike and three on the other—they'll need some revision. Met Cousin Sallie for lunch. Did laundry, charged my razor, etc., at her house while she was at her shop.

Palmetto Bay Marina was as low key as ever. It is rather plushly designed as part of a nice condo development with Woodie's restaurant the local's gathering place and a few other modern shops, mall-like under the five-story buildings The existence of a safe place to leave one's dinghy also makes it an easy-to-use link between boat and shore. But there are too few customers. How long can it all last? Saturday and Sunday, November ninth and tenth, went by in a hurry with all the necessary errands and exploring on the bikes. By Monday morning we were ready to leave.

Avoiding another unattractive stretch of the waterway, we departed from the southern tip of Hilton Head on Monday morning to sail down the Georgia coast past the mouth of the Savannah River, Tybee and Ossabaw Islands to St. Catherine's Sound. This 22-mile stretch of shore is all very shallow, demanding that I set a course three miles off, this time, to avoid a number of spots four and five feet shallow. The Loran began to give some strange readings indicating that we were five miles west of our intended course which was impossible, so we were maintaining three miles off by eye. As we approached St. Catherine's, suddenly we saw breakers ahead, and Ginger pointed to more breakers *seaward* of us! The centerboard was down and I felt it touch some sort of soft bottom as I made a violent left turn—probably in what is locally called "ploof-mud." The depth sounder slowly began to show deeper water as we backtracked northeastward before establishing a new course another quarter mile offshore.

We were fast approaching the St. Catherine's channel. Its mile-wide entrance between Ossabaw and St. Catherine's Islands was plainly visible though the islands were almost five miles away. According to the chart, from this position we should be right on top of a string of nine buoys to lead us in but there was not a buoy in sight. All we could do was to continue on, and continue we did for another two miles (!) before a buoy appeared, and three miles before we were close enough to read its number which was "5" instead of "7." Very confusing! Luffing up to search with the field glass, I could see only two more buoys. I could also see that this whole, broad entrance area was strewn with long streaks in the water made by powerful currents which not only can form long, shallow sand bars but can move these bars surprisingly long distances, especially during a storm. The Coast Guard must have had to move the entire array of buoys to this wholly new location.

Obviously, it's not wise to head into a situation like this until one figures out the latest arrangement, but at least it seemed OK to go to the two buoys in sight. When no more buoys appeared, I noticed that the chart showed a large deep area ahead so I plotted several courses on the chart to keep us within that area while also watching the depth sounder. Eventually two more buoys helped us avoid more shoals as we squeezed close around St. Catherine's north beach to reach Walburg Creek for the night. When I tried to crank up the centerboard I found that it would not fully retract into its slot in the keel. My quick turn in the "ploof-mud" must have bent that 500 pound, three-inch thick piece of bronze! It will continue to function but it could jam in the up position if I crank too hard.

Walburg Creek is a very narrow body of water which makes St. Catherine into an island. It seems always to be dark and somber because both shores are thickly wooded with sixty foot pines. Paleontologists say that human beings inhabited this island 2000 years ago and it has been used by Europeans since long before the civil war. Now, its only habitation is that of an extensive wild animal facility run by the New York Museum of Natural History with support from another ten history museums for the preservation of endangered species. Many rustic buildings have been built for tractors, labs, pens, aviaries, etc, all very neat with coarse but mowed lawns. The managers are very protective of their wards telling us that visitors are allowed only with previous arrangement and only on Wednesdays. We were allowed ashore only to explore among the remains of ancient tabby buildings, the great, tall pines, big spreading oaks and the large, silent spaces beneath them. Anchored nearby at night one hears all manner of howls, screeches and hoots.

In two more days we reached St. Simon's Island and Golden Isles Marina which finally has become as advertised. The big bascule bridge next to this marina is now permanently closed forcing the ICW to run west of Lanier Island, south around its southern end and thus forcing sailors to fight fierce currents back north two miles to the marina. It is part of a large, two-story, boutique mall with three restaurants and about fifteen elegant shops. Fancy! Fun to walk around. There's a barbecue outside under the overhanging second story serving hamburgers, or franks with beans for a dollar. Inside is a lively bar for beer and music. Every Wednesday the cafeteria has crab-legs—also for a dollar. After five o'clock it becomes crowded and quite lively.

The marina is full of local boats; the long, outer dock has power boats on the outside and sail on the inside, all very congenial. The dock master is both skilled and pleasant which we learned last night, when dense fog settled in and we listened on the radio to him talking boats around the long, southern shoal in the dark. No one knew about the bridge being permanently closed, and the boats were having all sorts of trouble with the currents as they struggled back up to Golden Isles.

This morning we pushed our bikes along the floating docks, thump, thump over the power-boats' 50-amp "umbilical cords," to the ramp. Then off across the bridge to St. Simon's. Ginger was terrified by the fast traffic on the bridge and highway. Not until we got to the rotary and the supermarket did the road widen enough to feel safe. We rode down to the lighthouse at the southern tip. Quite nice, and quaint— about 15 shops and the post office. From there we rode north past the small airport on a five-foot-wide bike path (good), detoured to the Atlantic beach and Sea Island before turning around and finding a nice, small mall for lunch. Though the bikes have small 20" wheels, they are amazingly easy to ride eight miles if one doesn't hurry.

FRIDAY, NOV. 15: Jekyll Island is next and as we approached its southern end, there were four boats pulled over against the shore.

Thick fog, blowing in from the Atlantic through wide St. Andrews Sound, was blotting out everything ahead in the ICW and there was a two-knot current running as well, so we joined the group and waited for an hour for the fog to lift a little. By studying the chart I saw that there were three buoys only a half to one mile apart to help one cross the sound's wide inlet in weather like this, and, by laying two compass courses, I could count on passing close enough to each buoy to see it no matter how thick the fog, and then finally head for Cumberland Island where the water was thirty feet deep right to its shore.

When the fog finally broke briefly, the big Hans Christian cutter retrieved it's anchor and headed out. That encouraged me, and thinking that I didn't want any more boats possibly getting in my way ahead of me, we followed. The Hans Christian's skipper veered a bit to the left of the course I'd laid and shortly slowed down. As we passed him in fog all around us he hollered, "You must be from Maine!" I saluted him while sticking right to my course because I could think of nothing wrong with it. Presently the steep shore of Cumberland Island materialized ahead exactly where it should be, and in another ten minutes the fog lifted and was gone.

We carried on all day to the Fort George River just north of Jacksonville where we found the Hans Christian, *Lahanna* at anchor. Fell into conversation about the fog, and soon Joan and Gordon Young came aboard for drinks. They are empty-nesters as we are; experienced sailors on their first cruise with *Lahanna* but their cruise is open-ended. They've sold their house and cars, told their children that they will keep in touch, and plan to cruise until they get tired of it perhaps many years hence. If we don't fetch up in the same harbor again along the way, we planned to meet in George Town, Exuma, in several months.

SATURDAY, NOV. 16: It is so nice to have comfortable weather instead of the unceasing cold of our first trip. Amazingly, most days reach 70° and no night has yet to drop below 40. Today was an easy sail to St. Augustine where anchoring is easy and secure. As we move south the landscape changes distinctly. North Carolina is pine right to the water or stark tree trunks in the open, scrub-covered marshes. Rarely any place to get ashore as the tangle at the water's edge would not support a foot nor allow through any animal bigger than a bird or snake. Dredged ditches are less common than forest-lined rivers and then there are the great sounds. There's no feeling of proximity to the ocean.

South Carolina is mostly ditch however, and one begins to see square-miles of marsh; light green or tan grass three feet high, its stems as straight as pins, and flat on top, capped at the distant horizon by a thin, dark line of trees. Occasionally there is just a little beachy feeling behind low, scrub-covered dunes. Next, the Wacamaw River, a true cypress forest of big trees sometimes standing in ten feet of water; daylight filtering through dappled shade.

Then the Georgia rivers: four hundred feet to a mile wide, deep to their muddy banks, winding aimlessly through enormous expanses of marsh. The dramatically vast "Marshes of Glynn." Mile after mile the ICW runs through tortuous, serpentine creeks connecting one river or sound to the next behind the large Sea Islands and many small ones with pine forests or huge, spreading, ancient oaks.

Florida arrives with a definitely beachy feeling. Far fewer trees but many palmettos and tall palms, clumps of low cedars. The dredging of the shallow rivers to facilitate the many boats have left dozens of tiny "spoil" islands which become very attractive when enough years have passed to allow small trees to cover them. Condos and houses now begin to crowd significant stretches of the long, barrier beaches which not too long ago were miles of orange groves. This land between the waterway and the Atlantic is often less than a mile wide.

We carried right on through Daytona—been there, done that—to New Smyrna Beach which looks nicer and has new marinas south of the old fish-dock section. The area between New Smyrna and Mosquito Lagoon is being upgraded fast by many, nice, new houses. The shanty fish camps are disappearing except in the small canals on the west side. The east side of the waterway is uninhabited; it's all dense, little mangrove islands, and between two of them we found a ten-foot deep space to anchor for the night.

By 10:30 the next morning Mosquito Lagoon was behind us and we were headed through the Haulover Canal on our way to Titusville's basin where we could get good ice quickly. Anchored for an hour. Easy dinghy access. Saw about twenty white pelicans and dense flocks of another bird, maybe starlings.

Hurricane Kate had come ashore on the Florida panhandle during the night so the weather has been uncertain for the last few days. We had good wind today, thankfully going southwest when south was forecast, but southwest made sense with Kate north of us. We carried a reefed main all morning and logged 5¾ knots into the wind unlike yesterday when, with no sail we were slowed terribly. Gray cloud masses are thickening overhead and a few spits of rain fell as we neatly skirted around the weather and came out into a fine afternoon and a great sail. No engine for the first time in weeks.

FRIDAY, NOV. 22: Anchored for the night at Banana River marker 83. By Saturday noon we were getting gas at "The Anchorage" where Barney has been dockmaster for years and lives aboard a trawler. He's retiring so we may not see him next time. On to that nice creek near the citrus dock for the night and then to Vero Beach on Sunday. Found plenty of space to anchor off that city's municipal wharf, park and dinghy landing. On a warm afternoon we dinghied up Bethel creek to Jaycee Beach and swam in the Atlantic. This whole trip so far has been improved by an almost total lack of winds more than eighteen knots. Most days have been like today with eight to twelve knots and temperatures around seventy.

Next stop, Manatee Pocket. Great to see the Horrocks again. They came aboard for dinner. Ginger womped up a full-course affair; roast chicken with all the trimmings which the Horrocks really enjoyed. The next morning Bill took me out to a radio-controlled model airplane meet. Controlling one of these things takes instant reactions combined with the ability to think right while acting left when the plane is flying toward you!

FRIDAY, NOV. 29: Departed from Manatee Pocket and sailed up the north fork of the St. Lucie River to Sandpiper Bay Resort where we joined the annual meeting of the Seven Seas Cruising Association. We are lowly associate members. To qualify as a full member, or Commodore, one must neither own nor live in a residence ashore. About twenty-five vessels from all over the world showed up for the festivities, including *Lahanna*.

Sandpiper Bay is a fancy resort for golf, tennis, horseback. It has a long pier at the north end of its thirty acres, many guest rooms and, of course, a big bar and dining room adjacent to branches of half a dozen well-known clothing, jewelry, and gift shops. There's an immaculate lawn sloping down to the river where we all dragged up our dinghies. None of us used the pier. This hardened bunch of world-wide sailors seemed a little out of place amidst such luxury. Many were somewhat unapproachable—perhaps a consequence of so many long periods alone at sea. It may take a true loner to adopt this sort of life year after year. However we enjoyed the opportunity to get to know the Youngs a bit. We agreed to meet in George Town in February or possibly late January

FRIDAY, DEC. 6, 1985: We've made some plans for the rest of this cruise. We want to take the Caloosahatchee River across mid-Florida in a leisurely fashion this time. Then we'll explore much more of Florida's west coast from Sanibel to Tampa-St. Petersburg, including Sarasota and Bradenton again. In the first or second week of January it will be time to head for Miami and across to the Bahamas for at least a month. We don't have to begin thinking about starting north before sometime in late March or even April.

The entire St. Lucie River is one of the prettiest parts of Florida. Both forks are wide and deep with a scattering of houses nestled in the heavily forested banks which slope up from both sides quite steeply. So much of Florida is flat that it's refreshing to see hills. The houses are substantial and many exhibit the work of an architect. Some look out to the water over gently sloping lawns to a dock and a large power boat. Only occasionally did we see a sailboat. We sailed down the south fork heading toward Lake Okeechobee and the Caloosahatchee for nearly an hour, passing these nicely landscaped houses before suddenly it became the St. Lucie Canal which is just that: high, straight banks topped by tall pines, live oaks and palmettos. Saw a six-foot alligator lying next to the bank, and in spite of hazy, gray weather we enjoyed the bird life and the landscape. Ospreys, king fishers, cliff swallows, turkey vultures, several different herons and egrets and, in the trees, a number of anhingas, They're the same size as a cormorant and rarely in the same area as the latter. Near evening there are huge flocks of turkey vultures, glossy ibis, white ibis, common gallinules, a wood stork, limpkins and coots.

By mid-afternoon we came to Indian Town, and this time we didn't miss the entrance. We tied up in a slip almost next to that which we occupied previously but no alligator this time. Sasha hopped off immediately and wandered all over having a great time. He fell in the water playing with a cat off another boat but jumped right out, shook, and went right on flirting with his new friend. This is farm country—tawny, dry grass fields begin only ten feet from the slips and run up a small, round hill where a dozen goats were grazing. We broke out the bikes and set off to the market about a mile away. At 4:30 it was swarming with Native American farmworkers. Ginger braved the crowd and heat inside while I stayed outside to watch our bikes where it was like Saturday night at the drive-in. The young bucks looked rough and were jostling each other around; I felt out of place. They were probably fiercely honest, but…who knows what little incident could explode into trouble!

Today, saw three alligators along the bank as we continued on our way to Lake Okeechobee. The Corps of Engineers had let its water level down at least four feet from where it was on our previous trip so there was plenty of clearance under the rusty, old railroad bridge. The notes in the log from the previous trip were very handy when it came to recognizing the various beacons leading across the lake to the so-called rim route. Long ago, dredges dug a deep channel along the edge of the lake and piled all the dredge spoil as a long berm on the lake side of the channel to protect it. Great, tall trees and bushes have since grown on it, enlarged and stabilized it. When we anchored for the night in their shelter we were swarmed by mosquitoes at dusk and all night. Be prepared! The lower water level left large, fuzzy balls of roots around the tree trunks and some trees were dying.

Again, there are huge flocks of turkey vultures here at dusk. They circle and "mush" into the trees for the night. At any one moment we see fifty or more. What do they find to eat which is so plentiful as to supply so many? Dead fish, possibly? We were quite annoyed by high-powered, little outboard boats, each carrying two fishermen. They'd roar past us at forty knots, stop in a rush of their own bow-wave, drop their hooks in the water for three minutes and roar off again. Was this a mosquito evasion tactic? Just before dark they all disappeared.

The next morning the Moore Haven lock came up sooner than we remembered from our previous trip. Locking-through is a non-event now. In a few more miles one looks out from between dikes to endless, flat, brown fields. There are almost no trees, no houses and this continues for sixteen miles, very monotonous until the first clump of trees appears marking our destination where we have come to visit our live-aboard friends, the Aikens.

Turkey Creek is the name of a group of small, short canals about eight feet deep, and a community to which all the home owners appear to have arrived by boat. They looked a little fierce and funky but turned out to be nice enough. One or two houses verge on being attractive but most are nondescript or are mobile-homes. I had a feeling that these men were blue-water wannabes whose bleached Westsails and homebuilt, steel vessels will never actually go to sea. The Aikins had only a dock and a storage room here; we helped Dave and Zora buy materials, put up insulation and sheetrock to finish it off. They were rather tense between expenses of building that large room and overdue customer payments for their writing and painting.

FRIDAY, DEC. 13: The landscape continued to be monotonous before finally giving way to patches of palmettos and scrubs, then woods at last. Again, I was surprised that the center of Florida could look like Texas. The town of La Belle is a reprieve; a neat farm town with a tiny face dock long enough for only two or three boats. Honey is a specialty, and their water is good so we filled our tanks. Shopping is only two blocks away, and La Belle Electric is an excellent plumbing, electric and hardware source of often hard to find products because it's primarily wholesale.

Now the houses begin to look more substantial and better landscaped. The first orange groves appear. The river still provides great anchorages in the little oxbows off the main channel and we poked into a nice one for the night with several trees producing the feeling that we were in our own snug hiding place. The next morning a couple in a Boston Whaler headed toward us; I thought they might chase us out, for some reason. But they introduced themselves as Buss and Diane

Hamilton and asked if we'd like to tie up in their big loop where we'd noticed four or five boats. They said they were about to start a low-key marina and would charge $10 a night including electric hook-up. After some discussion we took them up on it and moved over.

They'd recently bought the nice house here on twelve acres of lawn—Florida-coarse—and scattered trees. Diane is working hard on landscaping. Buss, a woodworker, is building a complete woodworking and repair shop and owns a fifty-four foot, steel schooner which he is about to bring down from Fairhaven (Massachusetts). He'd be very interested in storing *Lyla* for the summer, checking and opening it for ventilation, etc. I might be able to help him extend his traveling boom-crane so my mast could be pulled and stored out of the sun. Hmm. In the evening this quiet loop becomes quite a bird refuge. Again we saw gallinules, limpkins, anhingas, cliff swallows and coots in addition to the usual crows, gulls and mallards.

SUNDAY, DEC. 15: This morning was our first cold one. Forty-two degrees—but it warmed to 71° in Fort Myers. Tough! What a difference from our previous cruise. We are in Fort Myers Municipal Marina. Forty-five cents a foot including bowsprits or a dinghy in the water, an unusual attempt to squeeze a few more bucks from us. The piers here are all concrete, even the floating parts, a little rough on one's fenders. The best things about this place are its excellent marine store and its many, friendly live-aboards. A neighbor who is a local resident drove me four miles to the nearest kerosene supplier. Ginger had our Christmas cards Xeroxed. The nearest market is twelve blocks away; we don't need anything. Came across Lou and Bob Eberhardt on their Albin 25 again. Last saw them at Boot Key on Marathon in the Keys, 2/6/84. There's something wrong with staff's attitude here. They seem to *try* to be unhelpful.

MONDAY, DEC. 16: Negotiated the circuitous trip to Sanibel for more than three hours. Many markers and a succession of channels to be followed. But then a hidden entrance leads to a very pleasant, small marina in a park-like setting. Nice owners, mostly small power boats because many slips have less than three-foot depth. As we were heading for one of the deeper slips my jaw dropped; *there* was a Wasque

32 built by Vineyard Yachts when I was running the firm in Martha's Vineyard! I so informed the manager and the next day the owner appeared for a chat. Liz Lombardo, daughter of Guy Lombardo of swing band fame. Everything about this marina is good, and with bikes, both shopping and sight-seeing will be easy. Even Sasha likes this place. A good bike path leads to the famous, pure-white beach, and most necessities are available. Development is obviously accelerating but no high-rise yet. We need to come back here and spend some time. One might find a place to anchor but there are so many nice features at the marina that we don't mind the price at all.

WEDNESDAY, DEC. 18: Nice sailing today on our way northward through lovely Pine Island Sound. The wide open stretches were far more attractive this time with some sun, and warmth, and color. Helped pull a 30-foot sailboat off a spoil area near Green 53, then proceeded across wide, Charlotte Harbor to Boca Bayou. Here, one ties to a hedge of twenty-foot high mangroves which give protection from stray golf balls to the east. The other side, across the bayou, is all houses each with a private dock. We joined four other boats with an anchor to windward and a line to the mangroves astern.

The following two days put us in Bradenton Beach Marina which is only a short cab ride to Jane Gannon's nice, and very private, condo on a small pond right in the middle of this big city. There's not a sound nor any other clue that we weren't in a distant suburb. Jane is a close friend who spends all but a few winter months on the Vineyard and we will take over her condo while she spends Christmas on the island with her son.

In the morning we left the marina to back-track down Sarasota Bay and explore a little creek just off Route 41. We'd noticed it on the chart as we passed by on our way to Bradenton. It's only four miles from the airport and would be a mighty handy place to leave *Lyla*. Sarasota Bay, at this point, is very shallow for a half mile off shore but there was a channel dredged through the mud and delineated by a number of tall, unmarked, widely-spaced piles. Luckily there was little wind, the tide half-in and coming, so we poked along very slowly. Often, not knowing which side of a pile to try, we fetched up in the mud. But bit by bit we made our way in, finding five feet as we reached the shore and entered between two, six-foot high banks. Suddenly, we were in a small, hidden pond surrounded by six or seven houses and a Holiday Inn motel which faced Route 41, a hundred yards away. Several power boats were tied up by the houses, and near one end of the inn was a small pier but nothing else! Not a sign of anyone or anything moving. There was no road to the pier, only a path leading to the motel. We tied up at the pier and went into the motel to ask about using it. To our amazement no one seemed to know anything about it or to care. Even the manager seemed to think of it as something useless out back, while his mental focus was entirely toward the front of his establishment. We hung around, casing the whole place for a while and finally decided that if *Lyla* was anchored some fifty feet from the pier, no one would pay any attention to her. Even if they did, they'd need a boat to get to her. We called Jane to pick us up and she took us to her condo for the night. The next day we drove her to the airport for her flight to the Vineyard and stopped by to check on *Lyla*; all was quiet so we left her again to stay at the condo for the next week.

With a car at our disposal there was lots to do. We ran around accomplishing all kinds of supply errands in Bradenton which is a large, strip-developed, city. Items we hadn't been able to find elsewhere were available here. Explored the Bradenton waterfront one day. Its biggish marina seemed nice enough but the boats were mostly local so there were few people around. We prefer the Holiday Inn pond and it is free. Another day we drove north to St. Petersburg and Tampa Bay to see what that part of Florida might be like. It all looked too citified, too commercial to us.

Toward the end of our week ashore, my cousin, Nancy Parvin flew down from Connecticut for a week of cruising, and, on Monday, December 30th, after delivering Jane home from the airport earlier in the day, we three departed from the pond at 5:15 PM. It was nearly low tide at that time and we had quite a time getting out through the mud with the sun in our eyes making it difficult to see the pilings. After going aground several times, a *wading* fisherman, just a few yards away, pointed the right way to go.

We made it back to Sarasota just before dark. After passing through Ringling Bridge we bore right, into tiny Coon Creek to anchor next to Otter Key as we watched a magnificent sunset. In the morning Ginger and Nancy dinghied to nearby St Armand's Key, hid the dinghy under a low bridge and visited the fancy stores. I installed a new distributor and condenser, and replaced a fuel filter which was full of brown "dust." The engine had quit suddenly several times the previous day and would not restart for several minutes; not a good situation at all!

WEDNESDAY, JAN. 1, 1986: Moved to Sarasota's main anchorage and spent the afternoon at the Art Museum and Botanic Garden which are right on the shore close by. The engine quit again just as we were anchoring.

Thursday we started south and by late afternoon we were at the southern end of Lemon bay where the water narrows to a dredged channel through scrub-pine woods. Dense fog closed in, right down on the water as darkness fell. Gave up on our destination, Cape Haze Hole, and *felt* our way into a small, seven-foot deep bight across from Green #35. Couldn't see fifty feet ahead. This seemed to be a quiet spot and, in this fog, no other boats would be moving so we dropped our hooks. In the morning the fog hadn't let up at all, so I laid compass courses to each bend in the channel. Luckily there were buoys at these bends. Our big flash-light was useless; its beam just reflected off the fog without penetrating it at all. Anchored for fifteen minutes just a few yards from the big Gasparella swing-bridge because we couldn't see it *and* because this was the only spot to get safely off to one side of the channel. In fifteen minutes the fog began to lift, we upped anchor, tooted for the bridge to open and sailed out across Charlotte harbor. The remainder of the trip to Sanibel was uneventful except the engine quit suddenly several more times! I've found that it will start again if I wait about four minutes but this is not always the best.

MONDAY, JAN. 6: We've been in Sanibel for three days. Sasha is having a great time and disappearing for longer periods each day, full of play and happiness. One afternoon he came up on deck after a nap below, jumped off on to the dock, peered around, discovering a large bird on a nearby piling. He crouched...and, very slowly, he began to stalk it. As he got close, the pelican swung its big beak around to look down its long nose at this cat. Suddenly Sasha realized that the bird was twice his size, bigger than any damn bird he'd ever seen! He froze, arched his back, then stretched nonchalantly and ambled off just *slightly* faster than his usual walk.

Nancy is still with us so two bicycles are not enough. We discovered that the marina had a rather ancient car that we could borrow so first we took Nancy down to the lighthouse at the southern tip where we shelled on that perfect, white beach. The next day we drove all the way out to the north end and through Ding Darling Aquatic Park to the winter house of Vineyard friends for lunch. The five of us spent the entire afternoon exploring the amazing bird life in this park. Many of these birds seemed to ignore a quiet approach of human beings and would carry on with their fishing, mating, competing activities. For half an hour we watched a merganser duck make periodic, violent dashes through shallow water stirring up clouds of mud furiously with his beak and occasionally spearing his favorite fish. Following right behind him were three big pink flamingos feasting on the bounty of small crustaceans disturbed by the duck.

Back at the marina Liz Lombardo put me in touch with Mike, the local engine mechanic. I described how the engine would stop abruptly after running perfectly for half an hour and then refuse to start until four minutes had passed. He thought for only a minute before saying, "I bet there's a hairline crack in that old coil. So tiny that you can't see it. The coil works just fine until the engine heats it up and the crack opens causing the high voltage to fall. In four minutes it cools down enough for the crack to close again so you can restart."

Mike was right. The engine quit three more times on the way to Fort Myers where the marina had the right coil and the engine never stopped again.

After a night at Turkey Creek and another under the big trees near Clewiston we decided that the rim route around Lake Okeechobee instead of the direct route across it would be more interesting. There are high trees on both sides of this channel and most of it is wide enough to anchor anywhere until you get to the bridge at Belle Glade, a village which has the feel of one deep in the everglades. The small swing-bridge is hand operated. When we tooted, a tender walked to one end, opened the lock-pin, walked to the other end to do the same, then walked round and round pushing a capstan bar as the whole bridge swung very slowly open. A mile beyond Belle Glade the trees disappear and the channel joins the lake shore. In another hour we came to the Port Mayaca Lock, and in a few more hours we were in Indiantown.

Nancy sailed with us all the way back to Manatee Pocket where Bill Horrocks drove her to Stuart to pick up a rental car and drive thirty miles to the airport. Then he took us shopping to buy $167 of food for the Bahamas—enough for a possible two months. We did big loads of laundry and had both propane tanks filled. A full tank weighs about 24 pounds, is very awkward to carry and is too bulky to tie on to a bike. Rarely does a marina have propane, and the source is often a mile or more away, so when someone's car is available, I take advantage of it. Two tanks will last almost two months.

WEDNESDAY, JAN. 15: On Tuesday we left Manatee Pocket heading for Miami and the Bahamas. Spent a night in the little bight we call Channel 5 in West Palm Beach, and the next day we decided to stop in Fort Lauderdale because there are so many stories about it that we couldn't just sail right through it. From the chart we planned to anchor in Los Olas West. There's room for about twenty boats but, when we got there, it was crowded and Ginger wanted Sasha ashore so we turned east next to the huge marina, Bahia Mar Yachting Center. Our slip faced right into a nice city park so Sasha was given his freedom. However, this is all but *under* the Las Olas Bridge where the noise from tires running on its steel-grating road-surface was horrendous! The traffic is controlled by a signal so the noise would stop for thirty seconds but then begin again, a sequence much worse than a steady, uninterrupted noise which one might become inured to. The damn bridge was so close that it seemed right over our heads.

Long after dark, when the tide had gone out, Sasha returned to find the boat about four feet below him. He must have missed when trying to jump to the deck, because Ginger awoke feeling that something was wrong. She got up, climbed to the cockpit to find the poor cat clinging to a twelve-inch diameter piling, much too big to get his little arms around, and a three knot current swishing over him, all but pulling him loose. She grabbed the boathook, hooked the ring on his harness and saved him. One rat-like, wet cat! Ginger wrapped him in a big, fuzzy bath towel and began to rub him down. In two minutes he was purring so loudly that I could hear it over the bridge noise. No more than five lives left now.

Fort Lauderdale is a stupendous tangle of canals, marinas and boats of every size and kind, but mostly big, and all crowded together, many hundreds of them. Everyone who is anyone lives on a canal and, we've been told, some of them are beautiful. I have no desire to visit ever again.

Thus today, Thursday, January 16, we decided to avoid the crowded, traffic-jammed ICW from here to Miami by heading outside at Port Everglades, sailing down the coast twenty miles to Government Cut and thence down Biscayne Bay to our favorite Pines Canal. The passage was uneventful but slowed by the Gulf Stream current which seemed nearly as strong as a favorable, twenty knot wind, and also by the need to stay more than a mile offshore to avoid a plethora of shallow spots.

TUESDAY, JAN. 21: We've been in the Pines Canal for five days relaxing and waiting for a norther to pass. The wind has been howling but it's nice and calm here. This evening, after the wind dropped, we moved to Noname Harbor to facilitate an early start tomorrow. Lots of boats in this fairly large, nearly land-locked pond. Enough room to anchor but Pines Canal is much nicer and quieter. I guessed that only a few of these boats are headed for the Bahamas.

WEDNESDAY, JAN. 22: Again, as we did two years ago, we headed south to Fowey Rocks for a departure to Gun Cay. Again I established a back-range on two buildings behind us to determine the amount of course correction to counteract the drift of the Gulf Stream. However, now I could also check our progress with the new Loran. Long after the buildings disappeared the Loran read out the course to steer and the distance run. Gun Cay appeared dead ahead.

With lots more confidence than last time we pulled in behind Gun Cay which was only a little calmer than outside in the Atlantic but was fairly comfortable in the light wind. The next morning we motored over to Cat Cay to meet with the customs officer who, this time, did not leave his office. We wandered down among the condos where we met Bud and Doris Harris and Revis and Betty Stevenson who have a nice ketch at a nearby slip. The Stevensons invited us into their condo to watch the weather report on their TV. They urged us to push on, nonstop, to Nassau after passing North West Light.

So about six thirty in the evening we left in a flat calm to cross the banks. Saw very few boats on the banks all night. Had an uneventful sail in hazy moonlight and a glassy sea with the auto pilot steering the whole way. The Loran went ape a little after we'd passed Russell but probably because battery #3 was low. I switched it to charge and soon the Loran was OK again. I'd had too little experience with Loran to have faith in it so I took old-fashioned RDF readings which sort of indicated that we were on course. As we approached the all-important North West Light, I spotted its dim, red flash when still five miles away. Ahhh, my faith is rising. Let's now set in the Nassau entrance and see what happens. The wind came up just before we passed Chub Cay 2½ miles off to port and we had a fast six hour sail to Nassau, finally ending up close-hauled on port tack as the current across Tongue-of-the-Ocean set us toward the New Providence shore. Partly cloudy. We traded watches every four hours but didn't sleep much. Still, we were not so tired because of the help from the Loran and auto pilot. Quite a difference! When these things work, they *do* earn their keep. NW Channel Light was abeam at 0605, Chub at 0800 and Nassau entrance at 1450.

SUNDAY, JAN. 26: This morning we headed first for Yacht Haven for fuel as the engine has been on constantly since leaving Florida. As we approached the dock the engine overheated and I found water spurting onto the carburetor from a hole in a pipe-tee at the salt-water pump. The skipper of a boat next to us gave me a package of Epoxy-saturated glass cloth emergency tape which I wrapped around the still-hot tee and it hardened in fifteen minutes! Gasoline here was $1.75 but water to fill our tanks was $8.00 so we didn't top-off.

Sailed out of Nassau's long harbor about 10:15 headed for Spanish Wells on the north-east tip of Eleuthera Island forty miles away. As we were leaving we went aground at the Narrows Beacon near the east tip of Paradise Island. Our chart showed a course too close to the beacon while Kline's *Bahamas Guide* showed it correctly. The powerful current swept us sideways and pinned us exactly amidships against the beacon's pipe. I thought it would be easy to upset the balance a little and we would slide off. But after struggling to get free for fifteen minutes I called BASRA (Bahamas Air Sea Rescue) Their man in a Whaler arrived in ten minutes! He tossed us a line and, as I was wrapping it around the mast-base, we floated off, bumping over some coral but not brutally. I was embarrassed. I thanked the man and promised a donation to BASRA which is a much-needed and efficient organization run by American volunteers. The Bahamas have no functioning coast guard rescue service.

Turned north-west toward Chub Rock Beacon which is easy to see standing alone in breakers two miles out with Sandy Cay a half mile to starboard. From there we set a course to Egg Island where we are supposed to see the wreck of an old freighter as a land-fall before the tiny, low island shows up. Actually the freighter looked sort of like a light house when it popped up on the horizon, facing us bow-on, ten miles away. The Loran gave a good course and distance until we were about six miles away. Then it dropped from 57°, to 54°, 52°, and finally to 38° when we were only 1½ miles off. We were headed 15° to port of the freighter on starboard tack so we knew the Loran had to be way off. Back to old-fashioned piloting, but in a few more minutes the Loran seemed OK again.

Onward from there to Royal Island for the night and to Spanish Wells by mid-morning. The latter's well-marked but rather lengthy entrance looked very different from that on the chart, but it turned out to be easy to negotiate the narrow passage between the town and an island, and head for the small marina.

The town is compact, clean, neat, and populated by white Royalists. Besides a waterfront street, there are three more plus a dozen cross-streets. There's a definite bustle of commerce here, perhaps twenty automobiles, quite a few marine suppliers and the building trades: lumber, plumbing, electrical. The grocery, bank, drugs, liquor, etc., all looked well stocked. Yacht Haven Marina has more services than we've come to expect, is clean and even offers half a dozen motel rooms. At the waterfront there are a number of fast-looking fifty-foot power boats and we were told that there are many millionaires here, but they don't show it. Guess what produces this prosperity!

The anchorage has quite good shelter from the high casuarinas on neighboring Charles Island but it is tight. Five boats would fill it. Every space along the town's shore was taken. What used to be a shallow back entrance at the west end of Charles Island has recently been dredged to eight feet. The spoil piled up on each side can be seen for miles. We passed this entrance on our way to Yacht Haven, and there we nearly got into trouble with a strong, invisible current aimed directly into its slips. Though we entered our slip slowly, the current accelerated our speed. Full reverse barely prevented *Lyla* from crashing into the dock ahead.

Our primary reason for coming here was not Spanish Wells but a plantation on the main Island of Eleuthera named Sigatoo. A year ago, Ginger's cousin, Ned Collins, and his wife, Sue, bought this spread with a number of friends, all of whom will share it as a vacation hideaway. We have been invited to visit so the next day we motored across the quarter mile to the big island's north end to anchor in the lee of Gun Point—so named for the ancient cannon mounted there, ready to fire. We dinghied in to a little dock and walked another quarter mile where, up on a high promontory, is the magnificent site of a rambling old plantation house and three cottages set in three acres of old fruit trees and bushes imported from the South Pacific and the far east.

The plantation house is ranch style with gently sloping roofs, large overhangs shading the walls from the hot summer sun, and several wide porches looking out on picture perfect turquoise seascapes. The garden's several acres are a delight in which to wander and explore. Eventually one comes to the north edge, where spread out fifty feet below are the curl and sweep of small, white waves breaking on a long, wide beach. Ned and Sue were here just for an extended weekend, busy with many plans and work to be done, and obviously pleased with their venture, so we talked with them only for brief moments. We did spend a night in one of the cottages but we were nervous about *Lyla* should the mild weather and wind direction make a sudden change.

FRIDAY, JAN. 31: Projecting southwest from the northern part of Eleuthera is a ten mile long peninsula as thin as a knitting needle. It is cut through at its hilt by a narrow little channel aptly named "the

Current." Those words would be even more apt if followed by an exclamation point so it is best to pass through at tidal slack.

Some notes from the log book are a typical example of Bahamas navigation. "When heading for Current Cut, from five or more miles away, just pick out the highest tree-covered ridge and head for the right end of it where the texture of casuarinas ends and thick bushes begin. The charted beach area finally appears but the right end of this beachy shore is hard to see. Two prominent houses, high above on the hill, confirm this location."

Back aboard *Lyla* we left Spanish Wells just before noon in order to sail the crooked, ten-mile route through barely visible sand bars and arrive at the Current close to slack. Although we were only a half hour late, the current was already 2½ knots. *Lyla* was through and out the other side in a flash. Strangely the weather seemed to change on this eastern side. The wind was suddenly 18 knots out of the ENE and we were close-hauled starting across to the skinny neck of Eleuthera, and to Hatchet Bay fifteen miles away. The wind increased to nearly thirty and though we began to crash into the seas, *Lyla* had a comfortable motion. With the engine at 1350 rpm we averaged six knots in four foot waves. There was no lee until we were four miles out. At one mile the seas were nearly flat; we turned and ran down the coast for two miles. Most of this shore is steep-to and backed by high hills. *The Guide* says that the man-made Hatchet Bay cut through the bank is very hard to see. The beacon, high on one side of the cut was so small and thin that we passed it without seeing it or the cut before Ginger was pointing back asking, "Was that *it* ??"

Inside is a large, quiet harbor with all activity way down at the east end. A warehouse and fuel are along a rather bleak and forbidding concrete quay. No cleats, only an occasional big steel ring. It all looked scaled for the inter-Island freighters so we continued on to anchor just off a low, thatched building that turned out to be the local club and entertainment spot.

Ginger writes: "Hatchet Bay is a very good anchorage. Good laundry in the tiny village and a few stores. At the Hatchet Bay Yacht Club, Bernard holds forth at the bar, food is served, and the music—to the beat of first-class, live reggae—is loud and the dancing energetic!" We visited it one night—typical Bahamas down-at-the-heel—but pleasant and fun. Our white faces must have stood out in the dim light but we were heartily accepted. Ginger asked if they had Mount Gay Rum. "Sho, M'am, we got de Mun Gee!"

Another, somewhat unusual boat about our size is anchored near us, a Tom Colvin-designed, steel, junk-rigged schooner, *Contrast*, owned by Lyle & Jo Dean Jacobson. They too are headed for George Town, so we may see more of them.

The next settlement, sixteen miles south, is Governor's Harbor. Landmarks noted on the chart, again, are important here. The log book says, "Big clump of high trees which appears first is Receiver Bay. Its four radio towers don't show up until one gets close. Eventually the airport appears as does the white beach just west of the point. Next one sees the 'ball' on a hilltop which becomes a huge tracking dish and a high microwave tower beside it which you must aim for until you see Levy Island. An hour later you can see houses straggling from the water's edge to the hilltop."

The harbor is a big rectangle with one long side open to the Northwest. A single road, more than a mile long, which runs around the other three sides is no more than a dirt jeep-track. Except for the business section of town, only foot paths run among the fifty or so houses. Obviously, everyone walks. We saw not a single vehicle in the residential areas and only three in town. The road to the airport, several miles away is somewhat better but we saw no traffic on it. The populace has another habit perhaps because of the dearth of transportation; each house is surrounded by trash. The local disposal method seems to be to toss it all out a window and forget it. It's easy because most windows are fitted only with wooden shutters.

What do these people do to make a living, we wondered? The current answer seems to be, "They don't." When the British first came to these islands, back around 1600, they established Eleuthera and Governor's Harbor as the administrative capital of all the Bahamas. At that time many indigenous people from other islands were brought in to expand agriculture but the very skinny island, rarely a mile wide, was never able to develop sufficient export volume. In the 1950's the U.S.A. built a series of missile-tracking sites here employing a hundred or more central Eleutherans in addition to those employed in pineapple, citrus and tomato production, bringing a certain frugal prosperity to the island. But by 1980 the tracking stations all closed and, once more, farming had to shrink to that of supplying the Bahamian market alone. The tourist industry has recently grown a little but employment is insufficient, and many are left trying to survive on their own tiny gardens. "Enough of Eleuthera. Let's head for the Exumas," we said.

And so we did, sailing first across the open Bight of Eleuthera to Powell Point for an overnight and then on across Exuma Sound for thirty-five miles to Conch Cut which looked like an easy landfall.

The Exuma chain of cays rests on the east edge of Great Bahama Bank. It is almost 120 miles long and is considered to offer cruising delights second only to New England in summer. The hundred or so cays, most of them small and uninhabited, provide endless beautiful anchorages and harbors. There are so many of them that the spaces between are often too narrow to be navigable. We've been told that it is possible to cruise for days without coming to a settlement or seeing another boat. We had an introduction to the Exumas two years ago when we sailed to Highborne Cay. Now we are headed much farther down the chain's windward side in Exuma Sound, to Conch Cut and then on down the leeward side exploring on our way to Great Exuma, the Exuma's biggest island at its southern end.

The approach to Powell Point from Governor's is not easy. I would not have tried it without Loran. The Bight of Eleuthera, twenty-two miles across, has many sandy shallows which do not show as changes in the water color so one must plot compass courses to stay in deep water. Then, beginning about six miles from the point there are many square miles comprised of about a dozen, wide, parallel sand bores only a foot or two below the surface. They're invisible until one of them is so close that fetching up on it is likely before one can turn. The deep water in between is also wide and looks navigable, but most are dead ends a mile in. One must determine which is the last one and turn into it while still a mile from Powell Point. Then, having made your choice, you must spot an obelisk which will tell you two things: first, that you have correctly chosen the last rill; and second, the location of two submerged rocks which you must avoid. I could find no description of the obelisk. Is it like the Washington Monument, or is it the size of a small pipe? *Kline's Guide* spells out all the other information above with more than a page of diagrams and sketches; the *Chart Kit* devotes two pages and an aerial photo to this, but the two sources don't agree. Then the guide concludes with, "The Powell Point Marina is closed to visitors"—leaving our planning in a quandary. Back at Governor's I asked a fisherman we'd met about this. He uttered two words, "Drugs—Bad!"

Unfortunately there is no other place to pull in, and I didn't want to sail straight through to Conch Cut because we'd arrive too late in the afternoon to read the water. The photo in the *Chart Kit* shows another harbor only a mile away evidently empty and deserted—we'd try it.

With a great deal of uncertainty we made it through this maze. The last rill looked to be much wider than the others, and the obelisk, a white post barely visible from a mile away. The deserted harbor turned out to be a beautiful spot and very sheltered. In one of its three lobes there was a small forest of casuarinas where we dropped an anchor off shore and backed in to tie the stern to a tree. Sasha was allowed ashore, *Contrast* arrived, anchored in an adjoining lobe and all seemed perfect as we relaxed in the cockpit. An hour went by when a classy-looking jeep—a rarity in the Bahamas—drove through the woods; two men jumped out and called to us, "We came to help you. What is your trouble?"

I said, "None, we're OK."

They asked where we'd come from and where we were headed. One man stood by the jeep with his back to us. I guessed he was talking on a radio. Next, the other one said, "OK, have a good day," and drove over to *Contrast* where they told Jo Dean that both boats must leave immediately and go into the marina, "where we can watch you—not safe here; drug people around. We are security."

Wherewith, they drove off. They were Bahamians but they were well-dressed in stylish slacks and sport shirts. No doubt whose side they were on!

Jo Dean called on the radio five minutes later, all shaken up. We agreed that we should leave right now, move down the Exuma Sound shore and anchor out of rifle-range. We spent a rolly, uncomfortable night during which we heard a large, commercial-size vessel probably entering the harbor. A drug delivery? I was really irritated by being pushed out of that fine, comfortable anchorage.

WEDNESDAY, FEB. 5: We were more than ready to leave by 0700 hours. Set a course of 201° magnetic and dialed the latitude and longitude of Conch Cut into the Loran which agreed on that course. It was a nice, sunny day, a sky full of puffy little clouds. With the wind light out of the southeast, we were close-hauled into some chop and, as the wind increased, I was pleased to see that the Loran required 4° of leeway correction. Powell Point disappeared after 2½ hours and the auto pilot steered the boat all day. Up on one spreader I noticed its light was loose. I'll have to climb up there soon to tighten its screws. When the main luffed for a moment, the boom goose-neck slipped out of its fitting on the mast. I noticed it soon enough, ran forward to discover that the husky cotter pin had completely corroded away—a quick fix. Problems seem to come in threes so I was ready for the next one but it didn't occur.

A little after noon, land ho! Some little dots on the horizon. In an hour these resolved themselves into distinct shapes, one much bigger than the others which became the high, north end of Cambridge Island followed by the big, bell-shaped rock described in the *Guide*, confirming that the Loran had us aimed at the proper opening between cays. We zoomed through Conch Cut in a rush of current. Straight ahead was small, low Fowl Cay with a deeply indented bay, open to leeward. Looked like a secure place for the night so in we went, dropped our anchors and sure enough it was secure. There was a very nice house at the head of the bay, but not a person or another boat in sight anywhere.

The leeward side of the Exumas is mostly shallow since the "bank" extends for miles to the west and, the next morning, as we left Fowl Cay, sailing beside a very visible shoal, we had to go west for more than two and-a-half miles to reach deep water, a fathom. Then we had to stay that far west of the line of cays on a southeasterly course all the way to Sandy Cay before we could bear left to Staniel Cay. This cay had frequently been recommended to us so we were expecting first class facilities here. The entry is straight-in as one minds various landmarks to avoid shoals on each side, and there's a new Micro tower, 180 feet high, which is a bit to the north of the old one causing some error in the entry course given in the guide. The village appears to be spread out along the shore on several hills rising perhaps fifty feet. There is a marina at each end of it, each very expensive, we've been told. The designated anchorage, close to shore, was demonstrably rolly—we noticed more than one vessel rocking as we passed them—so we circled out beyond them to a grassy area about a hundred and fifty yards off where there was no roll at all. Not trusting the bottom, I dove on our anchors experiencing stinging sea-grass for the first time. It was no more than just unpleasant and, with a little care, I managed to push the anchors in to a quite firm bottom. The depth was only seven feet. We dinghied in to the "Yacht Club" Marina, walked into its clubhouse to find that it consists of just a very large bar, dimly lighted and nicely designed. A scotch and water was $5! (And remember, this is 1986.) At five o'clock there were so few customers that the place felt deserted.

The next morning we wandered into town consisting of about twenty—I'll call them cottages—half of which were part store, part dwelling made of rough, weathered wood and tin roofs. The two markets, Pink and Blue, are each just one small room with stock that filled less than half the available shelves. Pink has locally grown green peppers, tomatoes, potatoes, tangerines and perhaps fresh lettuce. Blue has staples, baked bread and may have frozen pork. For ice one must go to the Happy People—the other marina. At the tiny, basket shop Ginger couldn't resist a couple. For gasoline, it was back to the Yacht Club. No water available here and we couldn't be bothered returning to Happy People; we had plenty for another two weeks.

In the Bahamas we often dive overboard, then come back aboard, dry off slightly and rinse off in the shower below in the head to get the salt out of our hair. Should we still feel sticky, there's always Johnson's Baby Powder.

On Saturday we dinghied north about a quarter mile to explore three little but unusually high cays, the largest of which was recently named Thunder Ball because of its part in the James Bond movie. Putting on our snorkel gear we swam over to it, ducked under water to swim through a hole and surface in the cay's huge, interior chamber. It must be twice the size of an Olympic swimming pool and it's illuminated by sunlight streaming through a five-foot hole in the domed roof twenty feet above. I hoped that there was no one outside on top, who might toss a rock down the hole and hit us on the head! I couldn't resist swimming over to and wriggling through the small, submerged hole which Bond used for his secret escape. Met several American couples off other boats, especially "Trump" & "Crumpy" on a Triton named *Hayseed*, as happy and humorous as their nicknames.

MONDAY, FEB. 10: We left Staniel just before lunch for the easy trip to Little Farmer's Cay fifteen miles to the south. Dotham cut was abeam at 12:15 PM and for the remaining 11 miles we passed long, skinny Great Guana Cay which looks to be rarely more than two hundred yards wide. We had to motor directly into the light, prevailing, SE wind.

We are learning how necessary it is to spot every landmark as one sails along, because these cays often overlap and look like just one long island. From a mile away they all also look the same. Little Farmer's was easy to identify with its dock and cluster of houses spread over a hill. Now, we have to sail right on by it to avoid a series of sand bars and then, guessing when to make "a sweeping 150° left turn," take up a course of 22° which points us back at the tip of Little Farmer's, now a mile away. Then we are supposed to look half a mile ahead, over and beyond the tip, and notice a gap between two other cays in the far distance. We must adjust our position to one side or the other until our view of the gap is blocked by that tip and keep the gap just closed as we maintain the 22° course. By the time we had covered the mile, all the while jockeying around trying to keep all this lined up, we were, supposedly, precisely positioned to pass submerged rocks just off to port and a shallow, hard-to-see brown bar to starboard.

Ginger is forward on the bow trying to spot the bar as we slowly enter the bay enclosed by the three cays. We're being swept sideways by current and I must speed up. I steer sharply left to miss the bar and I holler to Ginger, "D'you see dark coral heads ahead?"

She says, "I'm scared, I can see the bottom!—Oh, the coral,—yes, right there ahead!" She points and I steer hard right as they slide by close aboard and more current sweeps us toward them. In another minute we are clear, and I can go left again to the town's tiny dock where we tie up beside several local fishing smacks. If you haven't followed all this, we are on the east side of Little Farmer's Cay, in a bay formed by two more cays farther east.

The settlement of about twenty small houses, all quite close together, looks attractive and neat. We ask a man carrying a garden fork where we might find the harbor master. He points to a small building near the top of the hill where we find Patricia, an English girl who, with her Bahamian husband, runs the Ocean Cabin bar and restaurant to which we have come. Enthusiastically, she fills us in on activities here and that we must anchor in the larger, second harbor, and, "how much does your boat draw? The harbor is all five feet. Go anchor and then come back at five o'clock when there will be crab races to bet on, and other American boatmen will gather here for drinks. Do you want dinner later? Let me know and I'll fix it for you!"

Then she sat us down to tell us her life story. She came from Hampshire and, after college, bummed around Europe with a back-pack for two years, then to the states but she was restless. On a cruise to Nassau she met this big, tall Bahamian, fell in love with him and craved the idea of a simple, island life. She realized he was smart and thought she could educate him. She would have him build shelves in their house for all the right books for him to read. He took her back to Little Farmers where she's been for eight years and where he has become the government's chief of this village.

There was one other boat, a trimaran in the big anchorage and, yes, all two acres of it seemed to be five feet deep. But it's quite sheltered by the cays all around. *Lyla* draws 3½ feet with the board up so we set our two anchors and felt pleased with the whole situation.

We joined the group at five. An odd assortment; one couple from Florida, another from Germany, two Bahamian men, Patricia and us having drinks and sharing stories. There was a strange sort of tension, running underneath that which is typical among strangers. I couldn't define it but later, Ginger said "It's boredom." She was right; a trapped and depressed form of boredom lying deep within each of the three residents of this place. It would creep out as a palpable futility discernible in the silences between their sentences.

The next morning, as we were wandering through the village, we came upon a group of teenage boys. Ginger began asking them questions about living on this island and I sensed some sort of violent reaction rising. Just then Patricia came striding up to us saying to them, "Hey, guys, why aren't you in school?"

They answered, "It's recess!" with a cheeky tone.

Pat turned on them, "OK, knock it off! Go! Down the road with you." And they began to straggle off. She turned to us saying, "They're too young to leave here but if they don't get away soon there's going to be real trouble." The older adults working in their gardens appeared more reconciled to the limited life.

TUESDAY, FEB 11: There's a nice breeze from the east so we're making good speed on a close reach. Perhaps we'll make George Town today, but if we don't we'll duck in somewhere along the way. It's 10 AM, kind of a late start when we have 40 miles to go. We passed through Farmer's Cay Cut into Exuma Sound an hour ago where, since the Sound gets deep quickly, we will be able to run the whole distance less than a mile offshore. The three-fathom curve on our chart runs as close as a tenth of a mile off shore, so we will be able to see many more details of this endless, overlapping string of cays than we did previously running on the banks. Some are low and almost flat, some have a mountain peak or two and taper off at each end. The peaks look like mountains though there's none higher than a hundred feet. Others stand out as a high and square white cliff. Most shorelines are low cliffs but, occasionally, there is a narrow strip of white beach. A few, tall, radio towers, an obelisk denoting some inlet, and a very occasional "prominent house" define our progress as we verify each on the chart. Of course the Loran confirms our position and reads out our speed as well. Excluding cays which are no more than a rock, we will pass about forty three today. Kline's *Guide* lists only about six as inhabited.

A while after lunch the north end of Great Exuma Island was abeam and at 1535 we turned in past Conch Cay which marks the entrance to George Town's big and beautiful harbor. It is formed by long and thin Stocking Island plus a few other cays lying a mile off Great Exuma for a distance of three miles. During World War II the Navy decided this was an ideal location for a large anchorage. There was even a hidden channel, seventeen feet deep leading into its SE end which continued at that depth for half a mile before shoaling to eight feet. There were also a number of shallower bars and a few coral heads so they began by dredging a few acres to eighteen feet and then continued to dredge the coral to ten feet for two square miles!

Now, on the west side of this harbor is George Town on Great Exuma Island where an encircling peninsula forms a snug cove for its marina, and a mile away on the east side, Stocking Island has three connected basins five to eight feet deep. There were fifty cruising sailboats here when we arrived; we were told that there would be sixty or seventy at the season's height. Stocking Island is famous so we knew that *that* was the place to anchor, and as we motored into its outer bay, there was *Lahanna*. We snuck right up alongside of them before they noticed us. Excited greetings! We rafted briefly and had drinks on board *Lahanna* before going off to anchor nearby. She is a large vessel, I believe forty-six feet, and very fully equipped for long term living and world-wide sailing with a wind generator, a fifteen-foot Zodiac and a windsurfer on deck. Below, I was surprised to see ten crystal martini glasses in cushioned, wooden overhead racks. They too have their sterling flat-silver on board—"It has to be civilized!"

On Monday morning we dinghied across the mile to George Town which took twenty minutes and felt like a long way because of our two-horse outboard and a small, but significant chop which insisted on splashing over the bow into the inflatable when we tried to speed up faster than slow. The water is as clear as that in a swimming pool; the bottom completely visible ten feet down when there's no wind. The town is the usual dusty down-at-the-heel, but has most of the common types of stores and better stocked than those at Staniel or Hatchet bay. The main street, unpaved but smooth, is just a block from the pier and right on that corner is a fine liquor store with very low prices. With all the boats in the harbor, the populace on foot was about evenly white and Bahamian. A surprisingly good library, a drugstore, a tiny restaurant, a dive shop. In another hundred yards up a small slope was the Peace and Plenty Hotel, a three-story building surrounding a patio which led to the bar and a swimming pool with a great view of the harbor; all very attractive. We'll be spending some time there. The other inn is less pretentious but still acceptable. The Bahamians seemed sullen.

We had a propane tank filled at the Gas Company for $8.50. There's a note in the Log, "Don't let anyone send you down to Bahama Electric Company where it's $11.50." The market is the busiest store and has a respectable selection but the prices are dear. Milk had just come in from the freight boat; we were told that it and eggs would be gone by Saturday and that the boat would not be back until next Wednesday. Film is sent to Nassau by Exuma Divers—one week and expensive. The only bank is almost a mile out of town next to the fancy Out Island Inn implying that the Bahamians don't need a bank. If this seems strange, it's not. Its business is largely U.S. offshore accounts.

Our primary mission tomorrow will be laundry so we were glad to find it right at the end of the pier. It's a long building containing ten washers and ten dryers plus two big, commercial dryers and it's a busy place where we met other sailors and gleaned all sorts of local info. Dinghies seem to collect in various places around George Town—under the docks, through the tiny cut into the pond behind the town at the market's float, at a small, low dock at Peace and Plenty, or mixed in among the locals' wooden skiffs. Speaking of which, every Bahamian waterman seems to be an expert at the art of sculling so every skiff has a deep notch in its transom. It's common to see someone standing in the stern, skimming right along, propelled by the action of one hand on a single, long oar protruding way astern. There are at least five anchoring areas and yachts move around constantly, depending on the wind, or a party, or shopping convenience.

WEDNESDAY, FEB. 12 through THURS, FEB. 20: Dinghied across again with the laundry and a batch of paper-back books. Ginger had loaded up two machines then walked down the street to browse and trade her books for another batch while the laundry got done. Back at the harbor several hours later the wind had come up producing enough chop to make our small dinghy difficult to handle. We managed to get only a few yards out before a wave broke right over the outboard; it conked out and we were quite wet with spray before I managed to row back to the pier. An hour later Blad and Judy Hansen took pity on us and offered to tow our dinghy back across while we sat in comfort in his fifteen foot Zodiac with fifty horsepower on its stern. Now I understand why these long-term live-aboards all have much bigger dinghies. Our outboard had taken water into its carburetor which had to be disassembled and allowed to dry out all night in the windy cockpit before it could be coaxed to start.

Rain off and on during most days. We are anchored some distance offshore in Stocking Island's main bay because, although the three lagoons are more secure, they are buggy! It seems to be prettier out here too and we're right in the midst of all the activity going on. A beautiful, little peninsula of the purest white sand I've ever seen protrudes into the bay and is used every day as a volley ball court until high tide covers it and erases all the footprints. Cocktails most nights with *Lahanna*; the ladies vying for best hors d'oeurvres—they're getting pretty fancy.

Snorkeled one afternoon about a mile down the harbor where there was pretty coral next to an ocean inlet. Joan came face-to-face with a six-foot shark—first time she'd found herself in the water with one—she turned, swam over to, up and into her Zodiac in one motion screaming all the way. Her thrashing instantly scared it away.

Bought good bread from "Little Toot" again. What a treat this is. Sue McGregor, a San Francisco girl who is married to a local diver and has two small children, lives high on the hill overlooking Stocking Island's second bight and bakes bread for the whole fleet. Just call on channel nine to place an order for your favorite kind and dinghy over to pick it up later in the day still warm from the oven.

Several times, we walked the trail over the Stocking Island hill to Exuma sound. It's steep down the eastern side leading to a mile of gorgeous beach like a small-scale Nauset on Cape Cod. Busy days with maintenance jobs and varnishing the toe-rails. Went overboard with flippers to scrub the bottom as it was collecting fine, green grass.

FRIDAY, FEB. 21 through FRI. FEB. 28: We anchored off Peace and Plenty one morning where we met Marion Murphy and the Youngs to tour Great Exuma in the former's car. Marion, an American who has lived here for 10 years provided an exceptional opportunity to explore this big island. Not only was a car necessary to travel from one settlement to the next—Steventon to Rolle Town—but along the way she'd stop to talk to many Bahamians asking about their doings that day and details of their lives. We asked her about the many deserted or half-finished buildings we saw as we traversed the single road along the island's spine. She said, "Some are built by whites who often can buy land cheap. But that's the end of 'cheap'. The real problem is the government. It has this scheme of taxing with tariffs, licenses, fees, etc. on whites *and* Bahamians, that when coupled with arbitrary, case-by-case application by local officials with absolute power, makes doing almost anything nearly impossible. People get started and then finally give up. Take buying a car for instance. No one can afford a new one because the transportation, the silly regulations and the license add up to as much as the car's cost. That's how 'they' pay for all those big houses on the hill back of Nassau." It is the mind-set that perpetuates this system which prevents the Bahama's economy from succeeding.

At lunch time she stopped at "Pieces-of-Eight", a partially open-air restaurant perched high on the top of the highest hill with magnificent views both east and west. There's entertainment at night—at each side of a small stage was one of the sound-system's speakers almost two feet in diameter! We were the only customers so we had the owner's complete attention. He and Marion were obviously old friends; she asked him, "How's business?"

"Same as always. No way I can build up this place with all the pay-offs every month!"

After lunch we toured the island's biggest and only commercial bakery. One long shed—just a high, tin roof on poles—keeps the sun and rain off the fifty or so workers and the dough-mixers. Two long lines of high ovens appear to be the shed's only walls. The aroma spreads for a mile.

The countryside is dry, covered with scrub growth and there are occasional clumps of green casuarinas. The villages consist of the same block or rubble-stone dwellings we've seen elsewhere. The kitchen is usually a separate building because of its heat. There's lots of open land; no crowding at all; here and there are tiny vegetable plots but landscape planting in any form seems non-existent. Hidden in a few scattered locations are quite posh resorts obviously designed by Americans, or perhaps by the British fifteen years ago. The Island has long sported the hideaways of the rich and famous. The Bahamians we met were very friendly. We've learned that the sullenness we experienced earlier disappears as soon as an individual gets to know (trust) you.

As Marion stopped to chat with a succession of women walking along the road, they greeted her with enthusiasm and she'd ask "Any casabas yet?"

"They's comin' but they want mo' water than I can carry now!"

Or, "Did I see that young James giving you a bad time last night?

Or, "All those sticks you've gathered. You need all that for your cook-stove?"

"My man said he'll bring home a lotta fish tonight. We'll eat and then I'll smoke the rest. I just hope he's gonna help me clean 'em all."

Saturday I ran along the Stocking Island beach and then body-surfed a bit in the waves while Ginger shelled. We took Sasha ashore for some freedom and exercise but that didn't work. First, when he trotted ahead of us we realized that the birds in the bushes alongside the trail didn't hide or fly away; they'd never experienced a predator. The moment he realizes this, he'll hook one. Next he came trotting back with the strangest gate; the sand was burning his feet. I gathered him up and slung him around my shoulders like a fur boa. Purr, purr. Sunday the surf was up and Gordon and I surfed for hours in six to eight foot waves. They curled a bit but gave us a great ride. Fun!

Had dinner with Ed and Barbara Collins on "Puck" from Michigan. We had met them at an SSCA meeting on the east beach. There are about a dozen SSCA boats here from all U.S. coasts, Canada, England, France and South Africa.

Monday I put new screws in the dangling spreader light, tried to fix the twenty-point light on the mast and we both did more, much-needed varnishing. Having filled our water tanks on Friday, I put ¼ cup of Clorox into the seventy-plus gallons just to be sure we didn't start growing grass or something.

Tuesday ushered in our second biggish blow; N.E. 20 to 30 all day. It began veering to south yesterday morning and came right on around by nightfall to west. We were pitching quite a bit and dinghying was impossible so we moved and found smaller waves under the steep north shore just far enough into the bay for more shelter.

Wednesday, all six of us convened for a fancy dinner on *Lahanna*. When Friday dawned as a beautiful day, we all went way down Elizabeth Harbor in the two big dinghies to Red Shank for shelling and sunning on the beach, then after a picnic lunch, across to Guana Island's good snorkeling reef before retuning to *Lyla* for cocktails. Later, a well announced cold front arrived and blew 25 to 40 knots out of the southwest. Since there was no associated low to change the wind direction, I let out more scope to produce less than a right angle between the rodes. The anchors held in that hard, flat coral which I feared would not allow them a good bite. The seas built up to three feet so we were pitching but not pounding. I should have slept well but I worried about our big canopy/ boom-tent and the outboard on our leaping dinghy which I should have removed. In the morning I found that, with elastic ties and no loose areas to flap, I needn't have worried at all about the canopy. We got the dinghy alongside still bouncing and hard to control in the seas, got a rope around the motor, loosened its clamp and heaved it into my arms. Then, we pulled the dinghy up over the stern and deflated it. Both operations were easier than I expected. Half a dozen boats came into our area, or on into the lagoons during this blow.

SATURDAY, 1700. Gordon, who has weather-fax equipment says this is now a huge storm so we will have S.W. winds for several more days. Aside from boat-keeping and a good de-salting scrub of deck and cabin-top with rainwater, we read all day. A bit chilly topside, and grey. Our first, all gray day in the Bahamas.

Lahanna started to drag so she hauled anchors and went over to Kidd Cove next to the "Peace and Plenty" for more protection from S.W. winds. Today Gordon heard the Coast Guard talking to Sea Lion about sixty miles east of San Salvador; sails blown out, engine out and taking on water. We saw them go out two days ago and we thought, "They must be crazy."

SUNDAY, MARCH 2: Met Bud and Nancy on *Departure II*. Ten of us on *Puck* for drinks. Later, after dark, we noticed many boats with their navigation lights on??? Turned on Channel 16 to hear that a Haitian boat had come into western Great Exuma and then was brought 'round to George Town. Ninety people on forty-one feet! They had had no food or water for thirty to forty hours, so two girls in a dinghy were going from boat to boat collecting food which they were going to deliver directly to make sure it all went to those in need. Also they were asking for boat-builder volunteers to help with repairs to the Haitian boat in the morning. Half a dozen skippers went to help.

TUESDAY, MARCH 4: The Youngs have left on their way south. Who knows how far or for how long? We have decided to start homeward since we will soon begin to run low on some supplies. Departed Stocking Island for Little Farmer's Cay. The day was thinly overcast with hot sun and hazy. It was easy to recognize the various islands from the landmarks, and I added more sketches to my previous notes on the charts.

Had a drink and hamburger at Ocean Cabin. About six boat crews were there for happy hour and crab races. Each contestant is handed a live crab and a narrow shingle. There is an eight-foot long chalk-line for the start and another for the finish about twelve feet away. You use the shingle to block the crab from going in any direction but the one you want it to take. With six crabs "racing," each with a name on its shell, it gets to be hilarious. The next day we explored. The town is spread all over a hill top, and near Patricia's house was a nice school building quite adequately equipped. One teacher, fourteen students, five grades, one classroom, one library with many Board-of-Ed-type books and nursery books, but not a single classic.

THURSDAY, MARCH 6: Warderick Wells is not to be missed. Twenty-five miles along Exuma Sound we picked it out with ease because we'd been told that a great pile of flotsam and jetsam piled on its highest hump can be seen from at least three miles. The north entrance looked easiest and as we made the U-turn around the point, spread out in front of us was a landscape of brilliant colors. A large, oval body of water was nearly enclosed by several small, hilly cays, dark green with thick scrub and a thread of tan cliffs at their edges. The quarter-mile- wide center of this lake was pure white, dry sand surrounded by two narrow, deep channels—two brilliant turquoise ribbons turning inky blue at their centers and winding their way around the white center. We passed three other sailboats in the main channel, continued on to a spot where the ribbon narrowed, and prepared to anchor. Standing at the bow, I could see the bottom clearly. As Ginger kept *Lyla* in position I lowered an anchor. It sank about six feet, landed on the gravely bank and proceeded to *roll* down its slope to the middle of the channel! Of course the anchor got tangled in its chain. I had to dive overboard, swim down twenty feet and carefully work each anchor well into the gravel. Can you imagine the strength of current necessary to form a sharp vee channel that steep? The hills were high enough to break the wind and provide a quiet night.

The next morning we dinghied a few yards to shore and hiked up to the landmark cairn. It's a pile of poles about ten feet high to which have been nailed driftwood boards, some with boat names carved in. There was a collection of bottles with messages inside, "Going to Caribbean? Please mail this." Another asking, "If you sail to England, post this message." Still another was written in French. The view from the cairn is magnificent—all the little cays wandering up the line as dark little lumps edged with bits of white surf, set in all shades of turquoise.

Highborne Cay was next. Approaching it from the sound side was a little more complicated than from the banks as we had before. It was just a convenient overnight spot so we left the next morning crossing on to the banks and setting a course for Nassau.

A beautiful, cool, clear day with a nice breeze. Sailed our courses with no adjustments. Went out from Highborne only two miles. The shoals are obvious and we were well clear of them by then. Sailed all day with the sheets more than eased and making six knots. I don't see why the *Bahamas Guide* says to go out four miles. Ran through one batch of heads just after noon as we crossed through Yellow Bank. Saw none that looked really shallow but with the water only twelve feet deep, we were wary. Landfall was a tower on New Providence; then a settlement to the right of it on the east end of New Providence. A half hour later the two casuarina clumps on Rose Island and "the gap" were visible; the latter very helpful to time the turn toward Nassau Harbor among that bunch of cays and rocks.

SUNDAY, MARCH 9: The wind piped up to 20, gusts to 30 during the night, so we were pinned to the boat; the harbor too choppy for our dink and many boats moved to our area from rougher places.

We rolled and pitched a bit, but not badly. Mostly sunny and cool. I cleaned the plugs again; it helped. They were lead-fouled again and covered with brown deposit. Leaned the mixture and worked on the autopilot. It has been acting up lately so I opened it up hoping to find something that I could fix. Inside is a loop of nylon string which links components of the steering mechanism. I found it wound twice around the little pulley, so I unwound and replaced it. Also wiped clean its compass electrical contacts. Discovered that *Delightful*, the boat next to us, was owned by Tom and Barb Miller. He runs the store at Whittaker Creek Marina.

TUESDAY & WEDNESDAY, MARCH 11 & 12: Departed Nassau for the trip across the banks to Gun Cay. Chub Cay at 1306 and NW Channel Light at 1950. Had a good sail to NW Channel but the wind was so light that we did not shut off the engine. Then the wind died altogether and there was no wind all night. The star reflections on the glassy water were fantastic, bouncing points of light. The wind finally came up about an hour out of Gun Cay and by the time we came to getting sail down and furled next to Gun Cay, it was up to 15 or 18 knots, SE. We anchored and *Lyla* began pitching uncomfortably. It was 6:45 AM; Ginger managed to cook eggs and toast and we fell into bed. In spite of being very tired, the pitching was just too much so we powered the mile to a quiet slip at Cat Cay. Just tied up, went below and slept all day.

The next morning we woke to music and noise. Cat harbor was much busier than usual. Turned out there were dozens of college kids on spring break, half a dozen on each of several, big, chartered sloops. The uniform of the day on board for most of the girls appeared to be topless.

THURSDAY, MARCH 13: Today we plan to sail all the way to Lake Worth Inlet at Palm Beach. It's 80 miles so we are off at seven o'clock and with the help of the Gulf Stream we should make it before dark. It's an absolutely beautiful day, cool with a SE wind at more than fifteen knots; scattered, scudding, white clouds in a blue sky and, *oh!* the color of that Gulf Stream—dark, inky blue, with big, snowy white-caps.

This became a wild ride with the seas increasing as the wind rose to twenty-five—ocean swells to eight feet. It was manageable because the wind was with the stream and we were running off. Hard to keep the working jib always full and when it re-filled, it did so with a nerve-wracking WHAP! When a big wave humped up slightly more astern than the prevailing wind, the jib would be momentarily blanketed by the main. Finally one of these shot the little pistons right out of four bronze jib-hanks and the sail had to come down before it destroyed itself. I had tried various whisker-pole settings and preventers to no avail. I just could not steer a straight enough course in those seas. But we were being dragged along "by the nose" at fantastic speed. Some of the rushes were spectacular! I put up the storm jib which reduced our speed only from *wild* to exciting; and so it went, hour after hour.

About three hours before we expected to reach Lake Worth inlet we made land fall of the taller condominium buildings along the shore and in another half hour the "tallest-of-ten"—as noted on all the nautical charts of the area—appeared to verify that our Loran was right on. The latter does make life simpler, but it also reduces the challenge of using every detail available to keep track of our position.

As we approached the inlet I started the engine. There's always the possibility that an inlet will be "boisterous" and that with the wind blowing into it, one could be caught in breaking waves, a potential peril to any slow-moving sailboat. The water of big waves in the ocean or a lake moves up and down but very little in any horizontal direction; thus a boat moves *through* the water. In the restricted water between two long breakwaters a sailboat may find itself in breaking waves which are moving as fast as it is, in which case there is no relative movement of water past the rudder, which becomes suddenly ineffective. The boat cannot be steered and is in danger of being swept toward the stones of a breakwater. Therefore, I wanted to be able to move through this inlet as fast as possible so I left the sails up and the boom held way out with a vang to add to the engine's speed. I'd take the sails down once we were inside. Well, we *did* get into breaking waves, the boat veered to one side, the rudder was not able to correct and we were headed for the rocks as the boat powerfully began to add speed. The vang, under tremendous tension, could not instantly be released. I grabbed the sheath-knife on my belt, cut the lines and the released sail swung free allowing the boat, now running across the waves, to answer the helm. I threw the knife below—no time to put it back in its sheath—one hand for me, one for the tiller. I was on the "downhill" side of the cockpit as the boat heeled from the wind and the now-sharp turn; *Lyla* just cleared the breakwater as she headed back out to sea! Upon re-entering I managed to stay clear of the breaking waves and entered OK. Whew! We almost lost the boat here. If I hadn't had a knife on my belt…but, hey, that's what it's for!

We'd not gone a hundred yards inside the harbor to where it widens out, when one of those long, narrow, overpowered, Cigarette boats came romping up along our windward side. Manning it were two young Coast Guardsmen.!? Through a megaphone, one of them hollered, "Stop! We wish to board you."

I hollered back, into the wind, "Give me sea-room to head up!" *You idiots*, I added under my breath. They followed alongside for a minute conferring with each other, then suddenly roared off. Perhaps one of them was telling the other that a boat under full sail cannot just stop, and that their boat was preventing us from turning into the wind. My guess is that the Coast Guard had caught that vessel running drugs and confiscated it. These two young ordinaries must have sneaked off with it for a quick, joy ride.

We got the sails down and pulled into Riviera Beach Marina to check in with Customs before heading to our preferred anchorage by Channel 5.

In the morning we motor-sailed north, up the ICW, past Jupiter Inlet and into Hobe Sound. The day was warm and humid, and a line of big thunderheads was building up in the NW confirming the weather report of a cold front moving in on us. Shortly after lunch the light SE wind veered to the west and died. Suddenly, less than five minutes later, came a violent gust directly out of the north. The temperature dropped suddenly from 80° to 65°. I had to rev the engine to keep *Lyla* moving ahead and then came the rain in torrents. The second gust built to forty knots, faded to perhaps fifteen, and then gust after gust, each shifting direction enough to keep me busy heading directly into them. After half an hour of this, the front passed over and was gone. In another two hours we were in Manatee Pocket where we went aground in the mud ten yards from Bill Horrock's dock. We had to anchor out in the stream until the tide turned and we were able to tie up.

The next day we sailed up the St. Lucie River so Bill could take pictures of *Lyla* under sail from his Boston Whaler. We had never before had a photo-boat to do this. We beat back and forth in twenty knots of wind as Bill maneuvered to get the right angles.

Afterward, we had a fast trip to Vero Beach as the wind definitely increased. With the wind aft, it was a bit boisterous for Ginger to steer and too much for the auto pilot also because we were on the edge of a jibe for most of the trip.

Vero Beach has added two red spar-buoys to delineate a new "Designated Anchorage" which will continue to be unlimited. North of this area one must show an anchor light and move elsewhere after seventy-two hours. The renovation work on the nice, adjacent park that was underway when we stopped here last fall has been completed. The great little dinghy dock on the side canal has been finished and there's no sand or dirt anywhere to track into your dinghy. No charge, either.

The weather is still partly cloudy and has been very windy each day except for two, short periods. Thursday we explored the very fancy stores on Ocean Avenue and then bicycled across the bridge to Vero Beach's primary shopping center where a good bookstore occupied our time for over an hour. Friday we had an excellent lunch with the Guys, old friends who'd moved here from the Vineyard three years ago. With the bikes it was an easy two-mile trip to their house.

Saturday the gusts were over thirty-five and we were pinned to the boat. With the wind so strong we didn't feel like dinghying the short distance to the little canal, especially with a slightly lame outboard. It may have gotten some spray into the magneto. We're writing letters, this log, etc., all day. All the boats are jilling around crazily. Earlier, we had to up anchors and move out of the way of a "junker" (an ill-kempt and old boat) which dragged down on us and had to be fended off.

SUNDAY, MARCH 23: We finally made it across to the dinghy dock getting only a little splashed. The outboard was OK again after I pulled out its main jet and allowed the motor to dry out overnight.

We took the bikes to the market and then to an art show in the city park. Bought a painting too large to have on the boat! The artist was willing to pack it up and mail it home to the Vineyard. The weather was still very windy but bright sun made it a pleasant day.

MONDAY, MARCH 24: Another good sail today. We covered the thirty-five miles north to The Anchorage Marina in five and a half hours. Barney was there to meet us at the gas dock and talked us into taking a slip. Later had a visit with him and his wife, Jackie aboard their trawler-yacht. He's retiring from the dock master job to Manatee Pocket. The Anchorage looks in first class shape. Did laundry and then visited the familiar stores in Eau Galle, a two-and-half block walk where we were nearly run down by several cars.

Florida drivers seem to believe that people who live on boats should plug the damn boat into a phone and shore power, and then rent a car immediately. Thus, anyone *walking* near a shopping center is fair-game and must promptly be run down. The streets have no curbs so they come chasing after you and you'd better be quick to jump, or even run, out of their way. Think I'm kidding? It's dangerous out there!

After another night in Titusville we headed for the Lighthouse Boatyard near Ponce de Leon inlet where we planned to be hauled out for fresh, bottom paint. The price was right for the haul-out there, and I would be allowed to use my own paint. Also, our heavy, bronze centerboard still could not be fully retracted—since our grounding in soft mud last fall—and this would be an opportunity to attempt to straighten it. Mike, the master of the yard's Travelift, lifted *Lyla* out of the water and, with the centerboard fully extended, swung her over the concrete apron. He then lowered her until the tip of the board touched the concrete and *Lyla* began to lean over as more and more of her 12,000 pounds rested on the board. I could see it begin to bend, but when he pulled the boat upright again, the board sprang back and there was no improvement. Succeeding attempts were no better.

Shortly thereafter the boat was propped up in the yard, men arrived to clean the bottom with a high-pressure hose and my work began. Life aboard a boat in a windy, dusty boatyard, climbing up and down a high ladder and using the company's only bathroom is not what I call fun, so I was determined not to get caught here Friday afternoon unable to be launched until Monday! By Thursday afternoon *Lyla* was ready to go back in, but there were three boats to be launched ahead of us and the Travelift didn't come for us until lunch-time Friday. By then I'd long since finished checking the underwater hardware and I was getting itchy about being left high and dry for the weekend! However, we were launched fifteen minutes before quitting time.

Spent the night at nearby Sea Harvest, the nice little marina at New Smyrna, and on Sunday, March 30 we made it all the way to the cement plant which is always calm but is only a convenience stop. Another rather ordinary day took us to St. Augustine.

The countryside has changed; we are definitely in north Florida, nearly in Georgia by appearances. Gone are the mangroves and casuarinas. Gone are the pretty little spoil islands. There are still a few beaches and tall, top-heavy pine trees, but now we pass vast, flat-topped marshes of brown grass tinged with spring green. Sometimes these panoramas appear suddenly from around a clump of trees, or form thin, brown lines under distant dark tree-lines along the horizon. The land is all but flat so the rivers and creeks wind aimlessly. The banks are coarse, gray gravel washed clean and bare by strong currents. Cypresses appear, and rounded, dense forests of oaks are just now flowering, leafing out in pale shades of green. Where there is less current, muddy banks may be crowded with oysters. Pilings have huge crops of them.

Anchors can be trusted to hold well in the heavy mud but they must be jounced and washed repeatedly before coming back aboard. Even so, the foredeck must be swabbed down afterward. We spent a pleasant day being tourists in St. Augustine, a quite nice city. Its Spanish heritage is apparent everywhere.

But then comes the stretch through Jacksonville Beach and north to the St. Johns River which we *don't* like. Dozens of snarling little outboards darting around at high speeds and unfriendly, absurdly expensive power-boat marinas. Nor do we look forward to the swamps beyond, so our plan is to avoid both by pushing quickly through to the St. Johns River and follow it eastward to enter the Atlantic at Mayport for a long day's trip up the coast to St. Simon's Island.

FRIDAY, APRIL 4: At 0600 the sun was just coming up as I stepped out on deck to get the anchors up. This early start will ensure that we enter St. Simon's Sound in good light and that we catch the fair current leading three miles up-river to the Golden Isles Marina.

By 0730 we were passing the big naval facilities at Mayport on a beautiful, still, early morning. Two huge container ships rumbled by, one sea-going tug and a few fish-boats comprised the only traffic. By 1100 we crossed the line of St. Mary's River entrance-buoys several miles off shore to surely clear several shallows on our northward course. With the wind light out of the east at about ten knots we had the big genoa up and the engine on to keep up our speed in the long, three-foot ocean swells. At 1505 the red and white, Morse-A outer buoy of the St. Simon's Channel was abeam and in another eighty minutes we were in the marina. What an easy trip with lots of fair current at each end!

Golden Isles seems to be running down a little. However, the bridge is quieter without the old steel grating surface, but the slips at the north end are still noisy especially when the Coast Guard, across the river, blares rock music. The marina will call them to turn it down which works until the next watch comes on. The bar in the mall runs full-blast, but the restaurant situation is inadequate, so we bought a pound of big crab's legs for four dollars to take back to the boat. Lots of bugs here this time of year and since we needed no shopping, we left the next morning.

We have had a strange rattling noise against the boat's bottom when we are at anchor at night. It has occurred several times in the last two weeks. It sounds as if a fishing line with a large, plastic lure on it had caught on the hull and was rattling against the boat's bottom by passing current. I've tried a number of ways to make it stop to no avail. Thoroughly mystified, I mentioned it to the dock master. He replied, "grunts. It's a noise that a fish called a 'grunt' makes. I know it doesn't seem possible, but that's what it is—just like a piece of sheet metal clacking against the hull. Maybe it's the fish's sonar."

SATURDAY, APRIL 5: Because we've been bothered by mosquitoes and no-see-ums lately, and because we are tired of the endlessly winding Georgia marshes we are going outside again to Hilton Head. "The Marshes of Glynn" are something to experience in good weather, but they can be wild, howling, bleak, and lonely in bad weather. Since it is seventy-four nautical miles, we first thought that we'd do an overnight but then we realized how easy it would be to duck into Walburg Creek for a night, half way along. After all we're not in a hurry.

The wind was light all morning after we set out but in the afternoon it piped up and we were anchored in Walburg just after sunset. The moment we stopped the bugs swarmed in on us and in the time it took to get the anchors down I've acquired more welts on neck and arms. I'll slather up with repellent before I go on deck in the morning.

The bugs seem to be less thick before sunrise and the current is fair then in St. Catherine's Sound so we're off early this Sunday morning. It was really rushing because this is the lunar-low tide of the month—four knots?—as we shot through the narrow channel and out into the Atlantic. It's mostly cloudy and the wind is east so I expect it to be stronger than that of yesterday. Again, we will have to stay at least two miles off-shore today to avoid numerous spots as shallow as four feet but, other than that, there's little to do except make sure the autopilot is on course and sail the boat. With a good breeze at fifteen or twenty, I'll be perfectly content doing just that.

Two in the afternoon—or 1400—we are just entering Calibogue Sound at the southern end of Hilton Head. The tide is lower than I've ever seen it. There are great sloping mud flats up from each side of the channel to the shores. The channel is very deep so I don't have to worry about going aground but I'm glad not to be in the small creeks of the ICW today.

1530 hrs: As Broad Creek cuts nearly across Hilton Head it heads east and we were hard on the wind. Rather than tack back and forth to Palmetto Bay we took the sails down and motored. The old schooner was the only boat anchored above the marina so we slipped in just down stream from her. The marina is still friendly and Chris was still on duty there. Had drinks with Tom and Annette. They seem busy with shore life and unhappy with Hilton Head but caught somehow. I think the schooner's maintenance is more than he can handle along with his job but he can't let go—a dream gone sour. Tuesday we had lunch with Cousin Sallie at her house and sat around discussing old times in New Canaan. Wednesday, the three of us went to watch some championship tennis: Steffi Graf defeating Chris Evert for the first time.

After all that wind from March 13–26 we have had more reasonable weather—like spring except no SW wind yet. The last few days have been the first typical—no more thunderstorms. It's easy to get started north too early in April and run into these storms with wind out of the north. If one just waits, there will be few, or no storms, and mostly SW or NW both of which are good. In the fall, the window to go south between the end of the hurricane season or prevailing sou'westers, and the beginning of northers seems quite narrow. Of course this varies from year to year, but I think that October is *the* month to go south.

THURSDAY, APRIL 10: Back in the marshes again. This has been a tiring day because the main was needed to help push us along through many strong currents, but it required constant tending to accommodate both shifting winds and looping passages of winding rivers. Fenwick Island on the South Edisto River offered space to anchor well clear of traffic in the main channel, and in good shelter from nearby high trees as well. Approaching my selected spot late in the afternoon, I got lazy and let the main sheet way out 'till the sail luffed completely and went forward to drop the sail. I let the wire halyard run just as a puff of wind filled the upper part of the sail and the wire jumped out of its pulley at the top of the mast and jammed. Oh, woe! The sail would *not* come down.

Ginger took the helm and I loosed an anchor which paid out and held as we drifted, thank goodness. But now what to do? The big sail was thrashing around; there seemed no way to control it, and the boat was trying to sail around the anchor. Ginger asked, "Why don't we try to braile it?"—which means furl it to the mast instead of to the boom. We did this and the boat stopped trying to sail. But there was no way to furl the part above the spreaders which was straining and ballooning like the upper half of a huge hourglass. I said. "I'll have to go to the masthead with some tools and pry the halyard loose. You'll have to crank me up with the jib-halyard winch." I got into our bosun-chair strop—a wide sling, actually—tied on a bag of tools and started up, Ginger cranking as I shinnied.

At the top of the mast, I had to hang on as it was waving side-to-side in wind that was stronger at forty-five feet above the deck. The halyard cable was deeply wedged between the big pulley-wheel and the side of the slot in the masthead in which the former rests. Bit-by-bit, with two screwdrivers and pliers, I pried it out and placed it back in its deep groove in the pulley while the sail tried constantly to jerk it out of my hand. The pulley fits so snugly into its slot that I found it hard to believe that the ¼" diameter cable could be forced in between. I'd broken a rule and relearned a lesson: "Never drop a mainsail when not headed into the wind."

A pretty sunset crept over this wide spot in the river as it curved through its gap in the forest, a palette of muted colors: olive water, black trees, spring-green marsh, mauve sky and a new moon with Venus next to it. The wind dropped and all was quiet except the current chuckling around the hull…until 2100 when a huge barge and its push-boat came thundering through the cut into our little bay. The pilot headed straight for us before turning at the last moment onto the range and rolling us in his bow wave. He probably didn't mean to scare us but needed the entire width of the channel to make the turn.

Two more days took us to Charleston and the Ashley Marina where we're now in a slip way up at the far end near the highway bridge, all by ourselves. The Wests are to arrive about 1600 to go cruising with us for a few days and this slip will make it easy for them to find *Lyla*. Shortly before they were due, we were below making up their bunks when someone hollered "*Lyla, Lyla?*" I stuck my head out of the companionway and there was John Farmela, a friend from the Vineyard. He had been driving across the bridge and, upon seeing *Lyla*, immediately turned around to seek us out. The Wests arrived shortly thereafter.

Northward, up the coast about thirty-five miles, is the small town of McClellanville. We had discovered it on a previous trip but had not had time to do more than a quick walk-through. Its harbor is occupied solely by big shrimp boats and the docks are all rotting away—not exactly a pleasant ambiance. But just beyond the waterfront is this charming village nestled among half a dozen enormous, old southern oaks with two antebellum churches of perfect proportions and leaded, stained-glass windows which glow when the late afternoon sun strikes them. Pat and Isabel were impressed.

We are following the prime of spring as it works its way northward each day. The rhododendrons are lush everywhere. It's so nice to see fresh, spring greens. Even the huge, flat marshes show a blush of light green under the brown top of the tall grass. Development continues apace all along the ICW, especially north of Charleston. Atop the Pine Island cut there are many more stores, and the wooded areas between watermen's shacks are filling in with houses at every income level.

Next was Prince Creek with its amazing echo and overhanging trees, a visit to Brookgreen Gardens for four hours, and then Hague Marina where the Wests called a cab for the short ride to the Myrtle Beach Airport. Just after lunch we decided not to waste another beautiful spring day and departed for Little River only about fifteen miles away. We arrived just as the sun ducked behind the tall trees which shelter this anchorage.

We anchored in our usual spot, but with six other boats. This time it was getting crowded! The Tahiti ketch, *Jeanie C.* out of Halifax, Nova Scotia was one of them. We had met her owner, Henry Mayo, two years ago at McClellanville. The current was 90° to the wind and we fore-reached all over after I put one anchor down while I watched before dropping the second. Henry hardly moved, nor did *Free Spirit*, a catamaran on our starboard side. After sidling from behind Henry to all the way in front of him, plus way out into the channel with our anchor way astern, I had to power backward before I could get 80 of feet of scope out and drop #2. This promptly stopped our wanderings and *Lyla* behaved like the ketch and the cat. However, two rather high-sided, thirty-five-foot sloops continued to wander in 360° figure-eights. Had a quiet night, woke to another beautiful morning, and didn't get hit by any vessels on one anchor.

SUNDAY, APRIL 20: Good to get into Sea Path. We were given a private slip again instead of having to stay at the long, outside, transient face-dock. As we were getting gas, the attendant said quietly, "If you people would like a slip, C-67 is available. No extra charge."

The next morning the wind was howling; gusts at least to forty so we decided to stay put. Strangely, in town it was just a light breeze.

Strange too was the sudden recognition that this might be the last time that we would play the part of visitors enjoying a strange town rather incognito, free to stay, experience and explore, or meet people or leave as we desired.

Tuesday was much colder with a north wind backing to south while many little cumulus clouds formed line squalls as we headed for the town of Swansboro for the night. The next day was cold again and we were glad to get into Whittaker Creek. Are we moving north faster than spring? We seem also to be foregoing exploration as we pull in to old favorites instead of ferreting out new places. Are we looking forward to changing parts in the play by going home, or reluctant to leave the present saga? We can't decide.

Took the courtesy car to the sail-maker to buy a new mainsail batten and, at last, replace the piston hooks in the working jib that had blown out during that rip-roaring sail from Gun Cay to West Palm. Then quick overnights at the nice anchorage near Wilkerson Bridge and the open marsh at Lutz Creek in the North River; another at Atlantic Yacht Basin, and a half day to go through the lock and continue to Norfolk City Dock—now called "Waterside"—part of the big, indoor shopping center.

Here, Ginger and Sasha took a cab to the airport and flew home to the Vineyard while I stayed on board to make ready for the three-day outside trip to sail *Lyla* home. Bob Sanborn, a downeast sea dog, nearly twenty years older than I, and Grant Foster, also very experienced, are expected to arrive tomorrow.

WEDNESDAY, APRIL 30: Bob and Grant stepped out of a cab about 3:30 PM. As soon as their gear was stowed below, they were eager to learn where every piece of equipment was located and how *Lyla* was rigged. In less than an hour they were satisfied and we departed for a short sail to Willoughby Point Marina which provided a bit more familiarization.

Our departure time the next morning was set by the currents in the mouth of the Chesapeake and in two hours we had passed under the Chesapeake Bay Bridge. The wind was light all morning as we awaited a coming front which blew in suddenly, switching from southeast to northwest and piping up rapidly to twenty-five knots. The engine was shut down and a double reef tucked in about 1:30. We were close hauled 'till midnight with moderate seas after which the wind shifted to west; no longer were we bucking head seas. The wind held all night and generally we had a fast trip all the way to Atlantic City the next day but it was tiring with the seas building up and the wind increasing to thirty-five as we passed the mouth of the Delaware. The Loran takes the work out of navigating but some of the fun and challenge are lost. No longer must we plot the effects of currents nor worry about the precision of our steering to ensure passing close enough to the occasional buoy to see it. The Loran tells us immediately when we edge off course. When I'm off watch I can sleep right through without concern about the next buoy because they regularly appear dead ahead. We still lay out the basic courses, of course, and note the important times in case the Loran were to fail.

Since none of us is in any hurry, and the wind and seas were becoming pretty boisterous we decided to pull into Atlantic City. The marinas there aren't very inviting; the biggest is state-run, has no fuel, no heads, laundry or ice but does have a restaurant close by. We could overlook the lack of the former features and a meal out seemed appealing. The dock master assigned us a slip in a rather awkward corner where wind, a bit of current and choppy water were all unfavorable making it essential to get a line around the up-wind, outlying piling on the way in to it. I nearly "lost" the bow from a wind-gust at the last moment but both men were good with the lines and full reverse stopped *Lyla* just as her bow-pulpit rode up on the dock ahead. It took some fussing with lines before *Lyla* rode the chop, the fenders resting against the float only in the gusts.

The tall buildings and glitz of downtown Atlantic City were only two blocks away but the waterfront is dreary, especially on a cold, windy, gray day. Everything looked run down, reminiscent of the Bahamas. Perhaps the restaurant would be more cheery so we set off to it—at least we wouldn't have to cook dinner. Well! It had all the atmosphere of a bus depot when no bus is due for hours. Big disappointment.

The next morning the storm was still at full strength. Blowing at least forty and it howled all day. Certainly not a day to go sailing—the seas would be mountainous outside. Walked to the supermarket where we were almost the only whites—the boys needed their favorite cookies, cheese and soft drinks. Scary area of tenements, two and three-story gray buildings and trash in the streets only a block from the big casinos. Back aboard *Lyla* we stayed below, reading and chatting in our warm cabin. As evening approached there was no way that any of us would brave that restaurant, and Bob's "famous casserole" cooking on the stove smelled great. Later the wind dropped and, after laying out our courses for the next day, we realized that if we started at first light in the morning, we could be in Vineyard Haven before dark on the following day. With both Bob and Grant as able sailors, a three-man crew plus autopilot is all that would be needed to man *Lyla* for even an extended cruise.

SUNDAY, MAY 4: It was dark and cold when we cast off; there was just enough light to see the buoys as we powered out of the channel and set sail outside in the Atlantic. Large, leftover rollers were coming in at an odd angle to the east wind. However, not long after sunrise, the wind aligned itself with the seas, the latter much bigger than they should have been. Before long, it veered to WSW allowing us to set a comfortable broad reach which we held for thirty-four hours all the way to the Vineyard Sound *Moaner*. By then, the wind had increased to 30 knots, and with a strong fair current running up the sound, the Loran was indicating more than nine knots over the bottom. The autopilot was doing all the steering—with the wind aft it could hold only 10° each side of our course—better than any of us could hold in these seas except when giving it 100% of our attention.

An interesting phenomenon occurred this morning, back sometime after we had passed Block Island. Suddenly we all had the feeling of being in home-waters, a certain relaxation from the inner wariness which is always present in *un*familiar waters. Though in an area of open sea, miles from the sight of land or buoys, we realized that each of us "knew" our position intuitively and quite precisely, in terms of so many minutes and direction to this or that. A long silence ensued, each involved with his own thoughts about this, the boat moving well and the sails steadily doing their work.

"Hey, are we being set inshore of our course a bit?" Grant asked.

"Yeah…could be," Bob and then I agreed. Each stood up for a look all around. No land, no buoys. "The torpedo range buoys are too far in for us to see, and we won't see the *Moaner* for over an hour but how about we tweak the autopilot?" Immediate agreement by all hands. An hour later the *Moaner* came up dead ahead. What was that certain, intuitive feeling that each of us had?—of knowing that we were being set off our course and not having the slightest inclination to pay any attention to the Loran. Just tweak the autopilot!

How rewarding it was to end our trip and our cruise with a rousing, fast sail up Vineyard Sound. We were home by 1830. There was space at the town dock so we tied up and hiked up to our house. Ginger exclaimed, "I *thought* you might show up tonight! The boys tossed their gear in our car and I drove them home to their wives.

Epilogue

During the summer of '86 again we struggled with re-entry. The sheer increase in the number of boats cruising the ICW, the crowding at anchorages and the anchoring limitations by land owners and law enforcement began to wear on us. The rarity of vessels kept truly "shipshape" and the new sort of sailors who owned them left us in a quandary. In addition, the furniture manufacturing business was demanding my full attention so we decided to put *Lyla* up for sale. An acquaintance who had dropped by occasionally in 1982 to check on *Lyla's* re-build made an offer providing that he could sell the Swiftsure he presently owned. After several months the sale was consummated, and he and his wife cruised her up and down the ICW for eleven years.

I was not all that pleased about letting go of *Lyla* and I needed some sort of replacement. During WW II, I had graduated from the U.S. Navy's excellent flight training program, and while I had not flown an airplane in forty years, one day I picked up a flying magazine wherein there was a picture of a small, single-place, kit-built airplane far more sophisticated than an ultralight but only double the price of one. A two-place version of such a slick, streamlined craft might be great fun! The possibility of owning an airplane, especially for someone living on a small island, for less than the price of *Lyla* was most intriguing. I called this little plane's manufacturer in San Antonio to ask, "Have you ever thought of producing a two-place version?" This wonderful southern voice came back, "We got it all deesahned!" By the end of 1989 I'd completed its construction, and in 1992 I flew it from Martha's Vineyard to California, eventually landing in 26 states. It was a fully-capable, cross-country aircraft.

Pages 104 and 116: The RDF failure in 1984 and the erratic Loran in 1985, both at Hampton Roads were caused by the U.S. Navy jamming the frequencies to protect its ships and facilities from Russian subs. Terrorists hadn't invented themselves yet.

Page 160: Sea Lion was lost. She evidently broke up in the storm.

Page 161: The Youngs cruised for thirteen years. We met them for lunch in 1998 in Newport, Rhode Island.

Page 167: Much later we *did* straighten the bronze centerboard. After *Lyla* was hauled for the winter in Vineyard Haven, she was resting in her cradle on beach-sand. The bottom of the keel was less than a foot above the sand so the two of us had to dig quite a deep hole before the board could be fully extended. Then, with rope, we lashed a 6x6-inch timber from top to bottom on one side of the centerboard allowing space for a six-ton hydraulic jack in the middle. After a number of tries pumping up the jack, bending the board and allowing it to spring back, we bent it enough to set it exactly straight. During that last try the board was bent so severely that I thought surely it would break!

Page 176: "That knowing feeling" is something that probably isn't experienced anymore with GPS, etc. That's rather sad.

Glossary

A range: Two marks, some distance up ahead or astern, which, by keeping them in line, enable a craft to follow precisely, a straight line to stay in a narrow, invisible channel.

Centerboard: A rather thin, retractable "keel" housed in the main keel which can be lowered to convert sidewise pressure from the wind on the sails to forward motion.

Chart Kit: a 17"x22" book of more than 70 navigation charts and many large photos of harbors.

Close-hauled, close reach, beam reach, broad reach, running off, down-wind are expressions designating the boat's angle to the wind. A boat is **close-hauled** when it is sailing in a direction as close into the wind as possible; thus with the sheets pulling the sails as close to the hull as possible. A **beam reach** is when the wind is abeam. A **broad reach** with the wind abaft the beam. **Running off,** or **down wind,** or **before the wind** is with the wind astern or nearly so.

Cringle: a bronze ring heavily sewn into each corner of a sail, and two more up the leach and up the luff of a main-sail at the reef points.

Dodger : A canvas cover on a metal frame over the companionway and forward end of the cockpit. *See front cover.*

ENE = east-northeast, **SSW** = south-southwest, etc.

Fathom = 6 feet. **Nautical mile** = 6076 feet. **Statute mile** = 5280 feet.

Green Flasher: Navigation buoys, when lighted, flash an identifying color or code at night, and a shape and color in daylight. Square-topped, green buoys, called "cans" will be on one side of a channel while red, cone-topped ones called "nuns" will be on the other. Often, instead of floating buoys, navigation aids are square or triangular, plywood shapes fastened to a tall piling comprising a **marker.** The sailor's guiding rule is, "Right-Red-Returning to harbor," or Retuning to Mile 1 at Norfolk. Thus one keeps red buoys on one's right when returning "home."

The head refers to a bathroom or just the toilet.

Head up: To point the boat up into the wind until the sails collapse and shake, or "**luff**," at which point the boat will coast to a stop. But only a schooner will remain directly into the wind. Others will fall away to one side or the other as the forward speed ceases.

Jibe: To allow a vessel which is running nearly **down wind** to swing from one tack to the other tack. Great care must be taken to prevent this from happening accidentally and causing great damage, in high winds even a dismasting.

Reef: A noun or a verb. To partially lower a sail and secure the surplus fabric along the boom with a row of reef points to prevent strong winds from overpowering a vessel. Our mainsail had two such rows, the lowest a **single reef**, the highest a **deep reef.** *See front cover.*

Rode: Anchor rope and chain of a small craft. On a ship, or large boat it may be called a **cable** even when made of chain.

Sachem's Head (SAY-chem's): A well-known, very attractive, small harbor near New Haven, Connecticut.

Scope: Length of anchor-rode or chain paid out.

Sheet: A line attached to the clew of a sail, leading to a winch and/or a cleat at the cockpit, to control and adjust the set of the sail

Tacking: A sailboat cannot sail directly into the wind or closer to the wind than approximately 45°. Thus a sailor wishing to go directly into the wind must choose port tack with the wind at 45° on the port side of the boat, or starboard tack with the wind at 45° on that side. Tacking from one side to the other, through the eye of the wind, he changes course almost 90° or a right-angle.

A **triangular sail** has 3 edges; **luff**, the forward edge; **leach**, the aft edge; and **foot**. It has 3 corners; **tack**, the lower, forward corner; **clew**, the lower, aft corner, and **head.**

Zodiac: a popular inflatable dinghy available in many sizes.

Charts

1: Cape Cod to Alligator River   p. 184

2: Albemarle Sound to Daytona Beach   p. 185

3: Florida and the Bahamas   p. 186–187

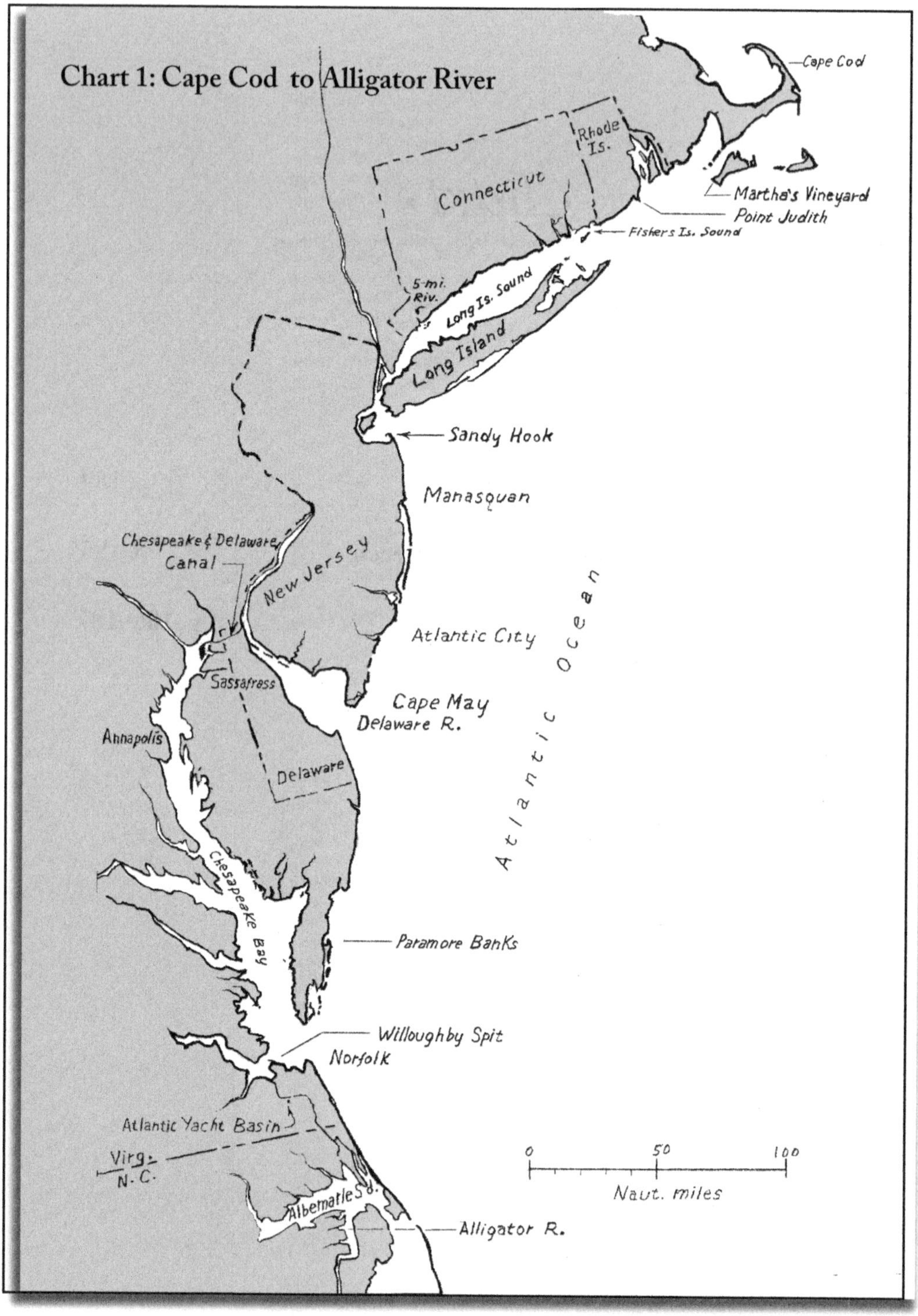
Chart 1: Cape Cod to Alligator River
Cape Cod
Rhode Is.
Connecticut
Martha's Vineyard
Point Judith
Fishers Is. Sound
5-mi. Riv.
Long Is. Sound
Long Island
Sandy Hook
Manasquan
Chesapeake & Delaware Canal
New Jersey
Atlantic City
Atlantic Ocean
Sassafrass
Cape May
Delaware R.
Annapolis
Delaware
Chesapeake Bay
Paramore Banks
Willoughby Spit
Norfolk
Atlantic Yacht Basin
Virg.
N. C.
0
50
100
Naut. miles
Albemarle Sd.
Alligator R.

Charts

Chart 2: Albemarle Sound to Daytona Beach

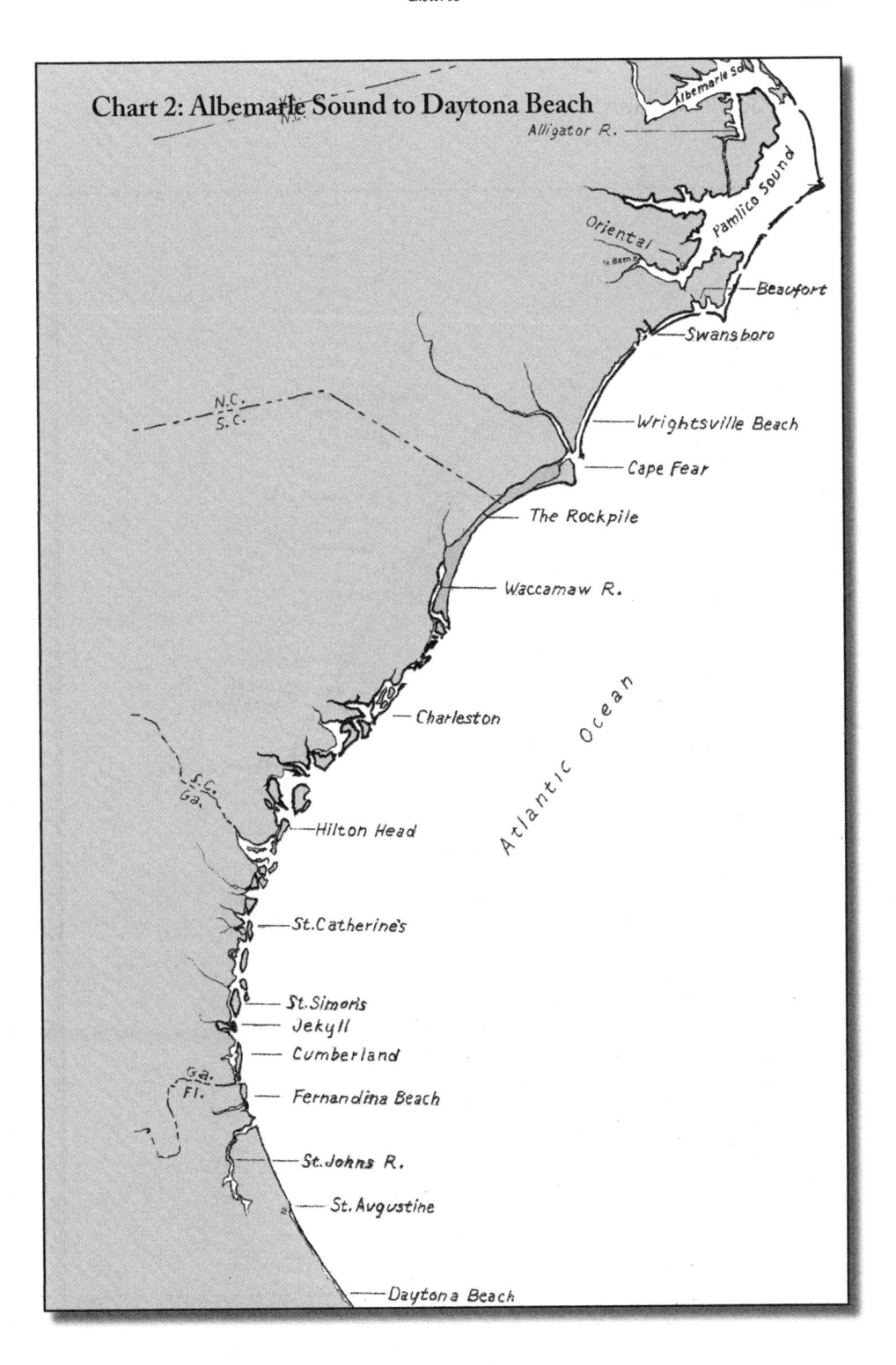

Chart 3: Florida and the Bahamas

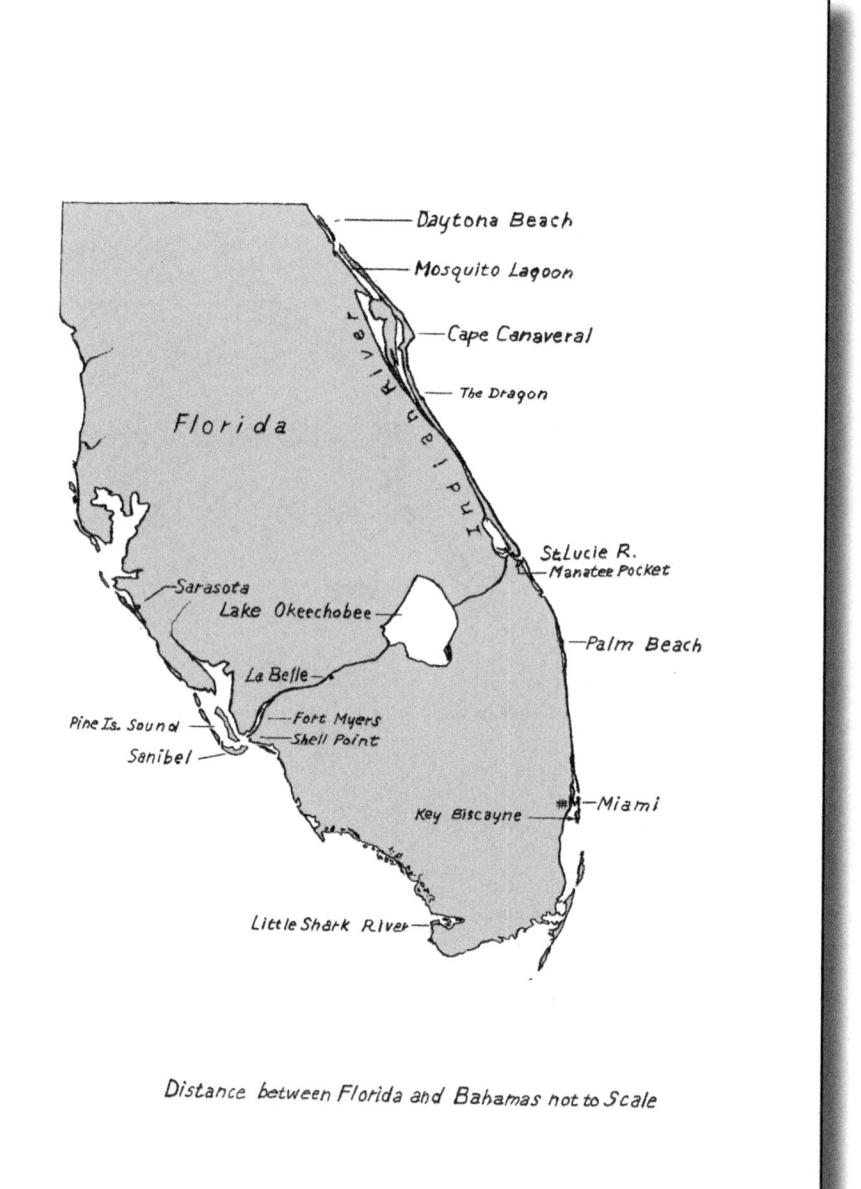

Charts

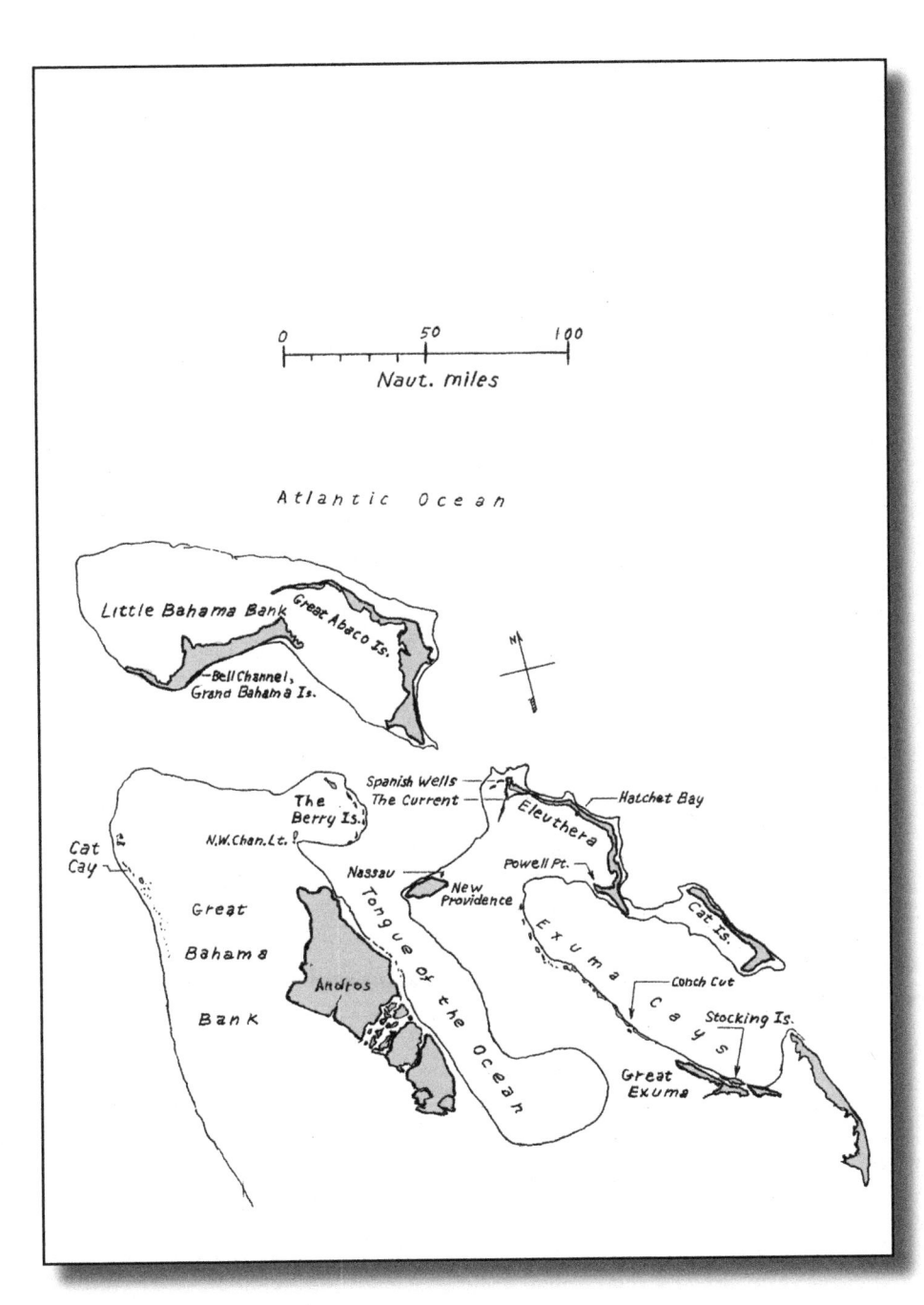

Made in the USA
Middletown, DE
09 June 2023